The conquest of Granada by the Spaniards. Acted at the Theatre-Royal. In two parts. Written by John Dryden, ... The sixth edition.

John Dryden

Eighteenth Century
Collections Online
Print Editions

Gale ECCO Print Editions

Relive history with *Eighteenth Century Collections Online*, now available in print for the independent historian and collector. This series includes the most significant English-language and foreign-language works printed in Great Britain during the eighteenth century, and is organized in seven different subject areas including literature and language; medicine, science, and technology; and religion and philosophy. The collection also includes thousands of important works from the Americas.

The eighteenth century has been called "The Age of Enlightenment." It was a period of rapid advance in print culture and publishing, in world exploration, and in the rapid growth of science and technology – all of which had a profound impact on the political and cultural landscape. At the end of the century the American Revolution, French Revolution and Industrial Revolution, perhaps three of the most significant events in modern history, set in motion developments that eventually dominated world political, economic, and social life.

In a groundbreaking effort, Gale initiated a revolution of its own: digitization of epic proportions to preserve these invaluable works in the largest online archive of its kind. Contributions from major world libraries constitute over 175,000 original printed works. Scanned images of the actual pages, rather than transcriptions, recreate the works *as they first appeared.*

Now for the first time, these high-quality digital scans of original works are available via print-on-demand, making them readily accessible to libraries, students, independent scholars, and readers of all ages.

For our initial release we have created seven robust collections to form one the world's most comprehensive catalogs of 18th century works.

Initial Gale ECCO Print Editions collections include:

History and Geography
Rich in titles on English life and social history, this collection spans the world as it was known to eighteenth-century historians and explorers. Titles include a wealth of travel accounts and diaries, histories of nations from throughout the world, and maps and charts of a world that was still being discovered. Students of the War of American Independence will find fascinating accounts from the British side of conflict.

Social Science

Delve into what it was like to live during the eighteenth century by reading the first-hand accounts of everyday people, including city dwellers and farmers, businessmen and bankers, artisans and merchants, artists and their patrons, politicians and their constituents. Original texts make the American, French, and Industrial revolutions vividly contemporary.

Medicine, Science and Technology

Medical theory and practice of the 1700s developed rapidly, as is evidenced by the extensive collection, which includes descriptions of diseases, their conditions, and treatments. Books on science and technology, agriculture, military technology, natural philosophy, even cookbooks, are all contained here.

Literature and Language

Western literary study flows out of eighteenth-century works by Alexander Pope, Daniel Defoe, Henry Fielding, Frances Burney, Denis Diderot, Johann Gottfried Herder, Johann Wolfgang von Goethe, and others. Experience the birth of the modern novel, or compare the development of language using dictionaries and grammar discourses.

Religion and Philosophy

The Age of Enlightenment profoundly enriched religious and philosophical understanding and continues to influence present-day thinking. Works collected here include masterpieces by David Hume, Immanuel Kant, and Jean-Jacques Rousseau, as well as religious sermons and moral debates on the issues of the day, such as the slave trade. The Age of Reason saw conflict between Protestantism and Catholicism transformed into one between faith and logic -- a debate that continues in the twenty-first century.

Law and Reference

This collection reveals the history of English common law and Empire law in a vastly changing world of British expansion. Dominating the legal field is the *Commentaries of the Law of England* by Sir William Blackstone, which first appeared in 1765. Reference works such as almanacs and catalogues continue to educate us by revealing the day-to-day workings of society.

Fine Arts

The eighteenth-century fascination with Greek and Roman antiquity followed the systematic excavation of the ruins at Pompeii and Herculaneum in southern Italy; and after 1750 a neoclassical style dominated all artistic fields. The titles here trace developments in mostly English-language works on painting, sculpture, architecture, music, theater, and other disciplines. Instructional works on musical instruments, catalogs of art objects, comic operas, and more are also included.

biblioLife
old books. new life.

The BiblioLife Network

This project was made possible in part by the BiblioLife Network (BLN), a project aimed at addressing some of the huge challenges facing book preservationists around the world. The BLN includes libraries, library networks, archives, subject matter experts, online communities and library service providers. We believe every book ever published should be available as a high-quality print reproduction; printed on-demand anywhere in the world. This insures the ongoing accessibility of the content and helps generate sustainable revenue for the libraries and organizations that work to preserve these important materials.

The following book is in the "public domain" and represents an authentic reproduction of the text as printed by the original publisher. While we have attempted to accurately maintain the integrity of the original work, there are sometimes problems with the original work or the micro-film from which the books were digitized. This can result in minor errors in reproduction. Possible imperfections include missing and blurred pages, poor pictures, markings and other reproduction issues beyond our control. Because this work is culturally important, we have made it available as part of our commitment to protecting, preserving, and promoting the world's literature.

GUIDE TO FOLD-OUTS MAPS and OVERSIZED IMAGES

The book you are reading was digitized from microfilm captured over the past thirty to forty years. Years after the creation of the original microfilm, the book was converted to digital files and made available in an online database.

In an online database, page images do not need to conform to the size restrictions found in a printed book. When converting these images back into a printed bound book, the page sizes are standardized in ways that maintain the detail of the original. For large images, such as fold-out maps, the original page image is split into two or more pages

Guidelines used to determine how to split the page image follows:

- Some images are split vertically; large images require vertical and horizontal splits.
- For horizontal splits, the content is split left to right.
- For vertical splits, the content is split from top to bottom.
- For both vertical and horizontal splits, the image is processed from top left to bottom right.

THE
CONQUEST
OF
GRANADA
BY THE
SPANIARDS.

Acted at the THEATRE-ROYAL.

In Two Parts.

Written by *JOHN DRYDEN*, Servant
to His MAJESTY.

———Major rerum mihi nascitur Ordo;
Majus Opus moveo   Virg Æneid. 7.

The SIXTH EDITION.

LONDON,

Printed for *J. Tonson*, and *T. Bennet*: And Sold by *J. Knap-
ton* at the *Crown* in St. *Paul's Church-yard, G. Strahan* and
W. Davis over-against the *Royal Exchange* in *Cornhill.* 1704.

TO HIS
Royal Highneſs
THE
DUKE.

SIR,

HEroick Poeſie has always been Sacred to Princes and to Heroes. Thus *Virgil* inſcrib'd his *Æneids* to *Auguſtus Cæſar*; and of latter Ages *Taſſo* and *Arioſto* Dedicated their Poems to the Houſe of *Eſt*. 'Tis indeed, but Juſtice, that the moſt Excellent and moſt Profitable kind of Writing ſhould be addreſs'd by Poets to ſuch Perſons, whoſe Characters have, for the moſt part, been the Guides and Patterns of their Imitation. And Poets, while they imitate, inſtruct · The feign'd Heroe inflames the true, and the dead Virtue animates the living Since, therefore, the World is govern'd by Precept and Example, and both theſe can only have Influence from thoſe Perſons who are above us, that kind of Poeſie which excites to Virtue the greateſt Men, is of greateſt uſe to Human kind

'Tis from this Conſideration, that I have preſum'd to Dedicate to Your Royal Highneſs theſe faint Repreſentations of Your own Worth and Valour in Heroick Poetry; or, to ſpeak more properly, not to Dedicate, but to reſtore to You thoſe *Ideas*, which in the more perfect part of my Characters I have taken from You. Heroes may lawfully be delighted with their own Praiſes, both as they are farther Incitements to their Virtue, and as they are the higheſt Returns which Mankind can make them for it.

And certainly, if ever Nation were oblig'd, either by the Conduct, the Perſonal Valour, or the good Fortune of a

Leader,

Leader, the *English* are acknowledging, in all of them, to Your Royal Highnefs. Your whole Life has been a continued Series of Heroick Actions, which You began fo early, that You were no fooner nam'd in the World, but it was with Praife and Admiration. Even the firft Bloffoms of Your Youth paid us all that could be expected from a ripening Manhood While You practis'd but the Rudiments of War, You out-went all other Captains, and have fince found none to furpafs, but Your felf alone The opening of Your Glory was like that of Light · You fhone to us from afar, and difclos'd Your firft Beams on diftant Nations, yet fo, that the Luftre of them was fpread abroad, and reflected brightly on Your Native Country. You were then an Honour to it, when it was a Reproach to it felf; and when the Fortunate Ufurper fent his Arms to *Flanders*, many of the Adverfe Party were vanquifh'd by Your Fame, e'er they try'd Your Valour. The Report of it drew over to Your Enfigns whole Troops and Companies of converted Rebels, and made them forfake fuccefsful Wickednefs, to follow an opprefs'd and exil'd Virtue Your Reputation wag'd War with the Enemies of Your Royal Family, even within their Trenches; and the more obftinate, or more guilty of them, were forc'd to be Spies over thofe whom they commanded, left the Name of *YORK* fhould Disband that Army in whofe Fate it was to Defeat the *Spaniards*, and force *Dunkirk* to Surrender. Yet, thofe Victorious Forces of the Rebels were not able to fuftain Your Arms Where You Charg'd in Perfon You were a Conqueror 'Tis true, they afterwards recover'd Courage, and wrefted that Victory from others, which they had loft to You And it was a greater Action for them to rally, than it was to overcome Thus, by the Prefence of Your Royal Highnefs, the *English* on both fides remain'd Victorious, and that Army which was broken by Your Valour, became a Terror to thofe for whom they Conquer'd Then it was, that at the Coft of other Nations You inform'd and cultivated that Valour which was to defend Your Native Country, and to vindicate its Honour from the Infolence of our incroaching Neighbours When the *Hollanders*, not contented to withdraw themfelves from the Obedience which they ow'd their lawful Soveraign, affronted thofe by

whofe

whofe Charity they were firft protected, and, (being fwell'd up to a Pre-eminence of Trade, by a fupine Negligence on our fide, and a fordid Parfimony on their own,) dar'd to difpute the Sovereignty of the Seas; the Eyes of three Nations were then caft upon You, and by the joint Suffrage of King and People, You were chofen to revenge their common Injuries, to which, though You had an undoubted Title by Your Birth, You had a greater by Your Courage. Neither did the Succefs deceive our Hopes and Expectations. The moft glorious Victory which was gain'd by our Navy in that War, was in that firft Engagement, wherein, even by the Confeffion of our Enemies, who ever palliate their own Loffes, and diminifh our Advantages, Your abfolute Triumph was acknowledg'd: You conquer'd at the *Hague* as intirely as at *London*, and the Return of a fhatter'd Fleet, without an Admiral, left not the moft impudent among them the leaft Pretence for a falfe Bonfire, or a diffembled Day of Publick Thankfgiving. All our Atchievements againft them afterwards, tho' we fometimes conquer'd, and were never overcome, were but a Copy of that Victory, and they ftill fell fhort of their Original, fomewhat of Fortune was ever wanting, to fill up the Title of fo abfolute a Defeat. Or, perhaps the Guardian Angel of our Nation was not enough concern'd when You were abfent, and would not employ his utmoft Vigour for a lefs important Stake, than the Life and Honour of a Royal Admiral.

And, fince that memorable Day, You have had leifure to enjoy in Peace the Fruits of fo glorious a Reputation; 'twas Occafion only has been wanting to your Courage, for that can never be wanting to Occafion The fame Ardour ftill incites You to Heroick Actions; and the fame Concernment for all the Interefts of Your King and Brother, continue to give You reftlefs Nights, and a generous Emulation for Your own Glory. You are ftill meditating on new Labours for Your felf, and new Triumphs for the Nation; and when our former Enemies again provoke us, You will again follicite Fate to provide You another Navy to overcome, and another Admiral to be flain You will then lead forth a Nation eager to revenge their paft Injuries, and, like the *Romans*, inexorable to Peace, 'till they have fully vanquifh'd

Let

Let our Enemies make their boaſt of a Surprize, as the *Samnites* have of a ſucceſsful Stratagem; but the *Furcæ Caudinæ* will never be forgiven 'till they are reveng'd. I have always obſerv'd in Your Royal Highneſs an extream Concernment for the Honour of Your Country; 'tis a Paſſion common to You with a Brother, the moſt excellent of Kings; and in Your two Perſons are eminent the Characters which *Homer* has given us of Heroick Virtue; the Commanding Part in *Agamemnon,* and the Executive in *Achilles.* And I doubt not, from both Your Actions, but to have abundant Matter to fill the Annals of a glorious Reign, and to perform the Part of a juſt Hiſtorian to my Royal Maſter, without intermixing with it any thing of the Poet

In the mean time, while Your Royal Highneſs is preparing freſh Employments for our Pens, I have been examining my own Forces, and making trial of my ſelf, how I ſhall be able to tranſmit You to Poſterity I have form'd a Heroe, I confeſs, not abſolutely perfect, but of an exceſſive and over-boiling Courage; but *Homer* and *Taſſo* are my Precedents. Both the *Greek* and the *Italian* Poet had well conſider'd, that a tame Heroe, who never tranſgreſſes the Bounds of Moral Virtue, would ſhine but dimly in an Epick Poem; the Strictneſs of thoſe Rules might well give Precepts to the Reader, but would adminiſter little of occaſion to the Writer. But a Character of an excentrique Virtue is the more exact Image of Human Life, becauſe he is not wholly exempted from its Frailties; ſuch a Perſon is *Almanzor,* whom I preſent, with all Humility, to the Patronage of Your Royal Highneſs I deſign'd in him a Roughneſs of Character, impatient of Injuries, and a Confidence of himſelf, almoſt approaching to an Arrogance. But theſe Errors are incident only to great Spirits; they are Moles and Dimples which hinder not a Face from being beautiful, though that Beauty be not regular; they are of the number of thoſe amiable Imperfections which we ſee in Miſtreſſes, and which we paſs over without a ſtrict Examination, when they are accompany'd with greater Graces. And ſuch in *Almanzor,* are a Frank and Noble Openneſs of Nature, and Eaſineſs to forgive his conquer'd Enemies, and to protect them in Diſtreſs; and above all, an inviolable Faith in his Affection.

This,

This, Sir, I have briefly fhadow'd to Your Royal Highnefs, that You may not be afham'd of that Heroe, whofe
Protection You undertake. Neither would I dedicate him
to fo Illuftrious a Name, if I were confcious to my felf that
he did or faid any thing which was wholly unworthy of it.
However, fince it is not juft that Your Royal Highnefs
fhou'd defend, or own what, poffibly, may be my Error, I
bring before You this accus'd *Almanzor* in the nature of a
fufpected Criminal · By the Suffrage of the moft and beft
he already is acquitted; and by the Sentence of fome, condemn'd. But as I have no reafon to ftand to the Award
of my Enemies, fo neither dare I truft the Partiality of my
Friends · I make my laft Appeal to Your Royal Highnefs,
as to a Sovereign Tribunal. Heroes fhou'd only be judg'd
by Heroes; becaufe they only are capable of meafuring
Great and Heroick Actions by the Rule and Standard of
their own. If *Almanzor* has fail'd in any Point of Honour,
I muft therein acknowledge that he deviates from Your Royal Highnefs, who are the Pattern of it. But if at any time
he fulfils the Parts of Perfonal Valour and of Conduct, of a
Soldier and of a General; or, if I could yet give him a
Character more advantagious than what he has, of the moft
unfhaken Friend, the greateft of Subjects, and the beft of
Mafters, I fhou'd then draw all the World a true Refemblance
of Your Worth and Virtues; at leaft, as far as they are capable of being copied by the mean Abilities of,

S I R,

Your Royal Highnefs's

Moft Humble, and moft

Obedient Servant,

J. Dryden.

OF
HEROICK PLAYS.
An ESSAY.

Whether Heroick Verse ought to be admitted into serious Plays, is not now to be disputed; 'tis already in Possession of the Stage, and I dare confidently affirm, that very few Tragedies, in this Age, shall be receiv'd without it. All the Arguments which are form'd against it can amount to no more than this, that it is not so near Conversation as Prose, and therefore not so natural. But it is very clear to all who understand Poetry, that serious Plays ought not to imitate Conversation too nearly. If nothing were to be rais'd above that Level, the Foundation of Poetry would be destroy'd. And if you once admit of a Latitude, that Thoughts may be exalted, and that Images and Actions may be rais'd above the Life, and describ'd in measure without Rime, that leads you insensibly from your own Principles to mine · You are already so far onward of your Way, that you have forsaken the Imitation of ordinary Converse. You are gone beyond it; and to continue where you are, is to lodge in the open Fields, betwixt two Inns. You have lost that which you call Natural, and have not acquir'd the last Perfection of Art. But it was only Custom which couzen'd us so long; we thought, because Shakespear and Fletcher went no farther, that there the Pillars of Poetry were to be erected. That, because they excellently describ'd Passion without Rime, therefore Rime was not capable of describing it. But Time has now convinc'd most Men of that Error. 'Tis indeed so difficult to write Verse, that the Adversaries of it have a good Plea against many who undertake that Task, without being form'd by Art or Nature for it. Yet, even they who have written worst in it, would have written worse without it · They have couzen'd many with their Sound, who never took the Pains to examin their Sense. In fine, they have succeeded; tho' 'tis true they have more dishonour'd Rime by their good Success, than they have done by their Ill. But I am willing to let fall this Argument · 'Tis free for every Man to write, or not to write, in Verse, as he judges it to be, or not to be his Talent, or as he imagins the Audience will receive it.

For Heroick Plays, (in which I have only us'd it without the Mixture of Prose) the first Light we had of them on the English Theatre, was from the late Sir William D'Avenant · It being forbidden him in the Rebellious Times to Act Tragedies and Comedies, because they contain'd some Matter

of

of Scandal to thofe good People, who could more eafily difpoffefs their lawful Soveraign, than endure a wanton Jeft; he was forced to turn his Thoughts another way, and to introduce the Examples of Moral Virtue, writ in Verfe, and perform'd in Recitative Mufick. The Original of this Mufick, and of the Scenes which adorn'd this Work, he had from the Italian Opera's: But he heighten'd his Characters (as I may probably imagin) from the Example of Corneille and fome French Poets. In this condition did this part of Poetry remain at his Majefty's Return When growing bolder, as being now own'd by a publick Authority, he review'd his Siege of Rhodes, and caus'd it to be Acted as a juft Drama. But as few Men have the Happinefs to begin and finifh any new Project, fo neither did he live to make his Defign perfect There wanted the Fulnefs of a Plot, and the Variety of Characters to form it as it ought, and, perhaps, fomething might have been added to the Beauty of the Stile. All which he would have perform'd with more Exactnefs, had he pleas'd to have given us another Work of the fame Nature. For my felf and others who come after him, we are bound, with all Veneration to his Memory, to acknowledge what Advantage we receiv'd from that excellent Ground-work which he laid And fince it is an eafie thing to add to what already is invented, we ought all of us, without Envy to him, or Partiality to our felves, to yield him the Precedence in it.

Having done him this Juftice, as my Guide, I may do my felf fo much, as to give an Account of what I have perform'd after him. I obferv'd then, as I faid, what was wanting to the Perfection of the Siege of Rhodes; which was Defign, and Variety of Characters. And in the midft of this Confideration, by meer Accident, I opened the next Book that lay by me, which was Ariofto in Italian; and the very firft two Lines of that Poem gave me Light to all I could defire.

Le Donne, I Cavalier, L'arme, gli amori.
Le Cortefie, l'audaci imprefe jo canto, &c.

For the very firft Reflection which I made was this, That an Heroick Play ought to be an Imitation (in Little) of an Heroick Poem, and confequently that Love and Valour ought to be the Subject of it. Both thefe Sir William D'Avenant had begun to fhadow, but it was fo, as firft Difcoverers draw their Maps, with Head-lands, and Promontories, and fome few Out-lies of fomewhat taken at a diftance, and which the Defigner faw not clearly. The common Drama oblig'd him to a Plot well form'd and pleafant, or as the Ancients call it, One entire and great Action. But this he afforded not himfelf in a Story, which he neither fill'd with Perfons, nor beautified with Characters, nor varied with Accidents. The Laws of an Heroick Poem did not difpence with thofe of the other, but rais'd them to a greater height; and indulg'd him a farther Liberty of Fancy, and of drawing all things as far above the ordinary Proportion of the Stage, as that is beyond the common Words and Actions of Human Life And therefore in the fcanting of his Images,

and

and Defign, he comply'd not enough with the Greatnefs and Majefty of an Heroick Poem.

I am forry I cannot difcover my Opinion of this kind of Writing without diffenting much from his, whofe Memory I love and honour. But I will do it with the fame Refpect to him, as if he were now alive, and over-looking my Paper while I write. His Judgment of an Heroick Poem was this, That it ought to be drefs'd in a more familiar and eafie Shape; more fitted to the common Actions and Paffions of Human Life; and, in fhort, more like a Glafs of Nature, fhewing us our felves in our ordinary Habits, and figuring a more practicable Virtue to us, than was done by the Ancients or Moderns. *Thus he takes the Image of an Heroick Poem from the* Drama, *or Stage Poetry, and accordingly to divide it into five Books, reprefenting the fame Number of Acts; and every Book into feveral Canto's, imitating the Scenes which compofe our Acts.*

But this, I think, is rather a Play, in Narration, (as I may call it) than an Heroick Poem. If at leaft you will not prefer the Opinion of a fingle Man, to the Practice of the moft excellent Authors, both of ancient and latter Ages. I am no Admirer of Quotations, but you fhall hear, if you pleafe, one of the Ancients delivering his Judgment on this Queftion; 'tis Petronius Arbiter, *the moft elegant, and one of the moft judicious Authors of the* Latine *Tongue · Who, after he had given many admirable Rules for the Structure and Beauties of an Epick Poem, concludes all in thefe following Words;*

Non enim res geftæ verfibus comprehendendæ funt, quod longæ melius Hiftorici faciunt · fed, per ambages, Deorumque minifteria, præcipitandus eft liber Spiritus, ut potius furentis animi vaticinatio appareat, quam religiofæ orationis, fub teftibus, fides.

In which Sentence, and his own Effay of a Poem, which immediately he gives you, it is thought he taxes Lucan, *who follow'd too much the Truth of Hiftory, crowded Sentences together, was too full of Points, and too often offer'd at fomewhat which had more of the Sting of an Epigram, than of the Dignity and State of an Heroick Poem.* Lucan *us'd not much the Help of his Heathen Deities There was neither the Miniftry of the Gods, nor the Precipitation of the Soul, nor the Fury of a Prophet, (of which my Author fpeaks) in his* Pharfalia; *he treats you more like a Philofopher than a Poet, and inftructs you in Verfe, with what he had been taught by his Uncle* Seneca *in Profe. In one word, he walks foberly afoot, when he might fly. Yet* Lucan *is not always this Religious Hiftorian: The Oracle of* Appius, *and the Witchcraft of* Ericho *will fomewhat attone for him, who was, indeed, bound up by an ill-chofen and known Argument, to follow Truth with great Exactnefs. For my part, I am of Opinion, that neither* Homer, Virgil, Statius, Ariofto, Taffo, *nor our* Englifh Spencer, *could have form'd their Poets half fo beautiful, without thofe Gods and Spirits, and thofe Enthufiaftick Parts of Poetry, which compofe the moft Noble Parts of all their Writings.*

tings. And I will ask any Man who loves Heroick Poetry, (for I will not dispute their Tastes, who do not) if the Ghost of Polydorus in Virgil, the Enchanted Wood in Tasso, and the Bower of Bliss in Spencer, (which he borrows from that admirable Italian) could have been omitted, without taking from their Works some of the greatest Beauties in them. And if any Man object the Improbabilities of a Spirit appearing, or of a Palace rais'd by Magick, I boldly answer him, That an Heroick Poet is not ty'd to a bare Representation of what is true, or exceeding probable, but that he might let himself loose to visionary Objects, and to the Representations of such things as depending not on Sense, and therefore not to be comprehended by Knowledge, may give him a freer scope for Imagination. 'Tis enough that in all Ages and Religions, the greatest part of Mankind have believ'd the Power of Magick, and that there are Spirits or Spectres which have appear'd. This, I say, is Foundation enough for Poetry, and I dare farther affirm, that the whole Doctrine of separated Beings, whether those Spirits are incorporeal Substances, (which Mr. Hobbs, with some reason, thinks to imply a Contradiction,) or that they are a thinner and more Aerial sort of Bodies (as some of the Fathers have conjectur'd) may better be explicated by Poets, than by Philosophers or Divines. For their Speculations on this Subject are wholly Poetical, they have only their Fancy for their Guide, and that being sharper in an excellent Poet, then it is likely it should in a Phlegmatick, heavy Gown-man, will see farther in its own Empire, and produce more satisfactory Notions on those dark and doubtful Problems.

Some Men think they have rais'd a great Argument against the use of Spectres and Magick in Heroick Poetry, by saying, they are unnatural; but, whether they or I believe there are such things, is not material; 'tis enough, that for ought we know, they may be in Nature, and whatever is, or may be, is not properly unnatural. Neither am I much concern'd at Mr. Cowley's Verses before Gondibert, (though his Authority is almost Sacred to me·) 'Tis true, he has resembled the old Epick Poetry to a Fantastick Fairy-land, but he has contradicted himself by his own Example. For he has himself made use of Angels and Visions in his Davideis, as well as Tasso in his Godfrey.

What I have written on this Subject will not be thought Digression by the Reader, if he please to remember what I said in the beginning of this Essay, that I have modell'd my Heroick Plays by the Rules of an Heroick Poem. And if that be the most noble, the most pleasant, and the most instructive way of writing in Verse, and, withal, the highest Pattern of Human Life, as all Poets have agreed, I shall need no other Argument to justifie my Choice in this Imitation. One Advantage the Drama has above the other, namely, that it represents to View what the Poem only does relate, and, Segnius irritant animum demissa per aures, Quam quæ sunt oculis subjecta fidelibus, as Horace tells us.

To those who object my frequent use of Drums and Trumpets, and my Representations of Battels; I answer, I introduc'd them not on the English

Stage;

Stage; Shakefpear us'd them frequently; and though Johnfon fhews no Battel in his Cataline, yet you hear from behind the Scenes the founding of Trumpets, and the Shouts of fighting Armies. But, I add farther; that thefe Warlike Inftruments, and even their Prefentations of fighting on the Stage, are no more than neceffary to produce the Effects of an Heroick Play; that is, to raife the Imagination of the Audience, and to perfuade them, for the time, that what they behold on the Theatre is really perform'd. The Poet is then to endeavour an abfolute Dominion over the Minds of the Spectators; for, though our Fancy will contribute to its own Deceit, yet a Writer ought to help its Operation. And that the Red Bull has formerly done the fame, is no more an Argument againft our Practice, than it would be for a Phyfician to forbear an approv'd Medicine, becaufe a Mountebank has us'd it with Succefs.

Thus I have given a fhort Account of Heroick Plays. I might now, with the ufual Eagernefs of an Author, make a particular Defence of this. But the common Opinion (how unjuft foever) has been fo much to my Advantage, that I have reafon to be fatisfy'd, and to fuffer with Patience all that can be urg'd againft it.

For, otherwife, what can be more eafie for me, than to defend the Character of Almanzor, which is one great Exception that is made againft the Play? 'Tis faid, that Almanzor is no perfect Pattern of Heroick Virtue, that he is a Contemner of Kings, and that he is made to perform Impoffibilities.

I muft therefore avow, in the firft place, from whence I took the Character. The firft Image I had of him, was from the Achilles of Homer, the next from Taffo's Rinaldo, (who was a Copy of the former) and the third from the Artaban of Monfieur Calpranede, (who has imitated both.) The Original of thefe (Achilles) is taken by Homer for his Heroe; and is defcrib'd by him as one, who in Strength and Courage furpafs'd the reft of the Grecian Army, but, withal, of fo fiery a Temper, fo impatient of an Injury, even from his King and General, that when his Miftrefs was to be forc'd from him by the Command of Agamemnon, he not only difobey'd it, but return'd him an Anfwer full of Contumely, and in the moft opprobrious Terms he could imagine; they are Homer's Words which follow, and I have cited but fome few amongft a Multitude.

Οἰνοβαρὲς, κυνὸς ὄμματ' ἔχων, κραδίην δ' ἐλάφοιο   Il. α. v. 225.
Δημοβόρ⊙ βασιλεὺς, Il. α. v. 321.

Nay, he proceeded fo far in his Infolence, as to draw out his Sword, with Intention to kill him,

Ἕλκετο δ' ἐκ κολεοῖο μέγα ξίφ⊙. Il. α. v 194.

and if Minerva had not appear'd, and held his Hand, he had executed his Defign; and 'twas all fhe could do to diffuade him from it.   The Event
was,

was, that he left the Army, and would fight no more. Agamemnon *gives his Character thus to* Nestor;

Ἀλλ' ὅδ' ἀνὴρ ἐθέλῃ ϖεὶ πάντων ἔμμεναι ἄλλων II. α. v. 287, 288
Πάντων μὲν κρατέειν ἐθέλῃ, πάντεσι δ' ἀνάσσειν

and Horace *gives the same Description of him in his Art of Poetry.*

———Honoratum si forte reponis Achillem,
Impiger, Iracundus, Inexorabilis, Acer,
Jura neget sibi nata, nihil non arroget armis.

Tasso's *chief Character,* Rinaldo, *was a Man of the same Temper; for, when he had Slain* Gernando *in his heat of Passion, he not only refus'd to be judg'd by* Godfrey, *his General, but threaten'd, that if he came to seize him, he would right himself by Arms upon him; witness these following Lines of* Tasso.

Venga, egli omandi, jo terro fermo il piede;
Giudici fian tra noi la forte, e'l arme.
Fera tragedia vuol che s'apprefenti
Per los diporti a le Nemiche genti.

You see how little these great Authors did esteem the Point of Honour, so much magnify'd by the French, *and so ridiculously ap'd by us. They made their Heroes* Men of Honour; *but so, as not to divest them quite of Human Passions and Frailties, they content themselves to shew you, what Men of great Spirits would certainly do when they were provok'd, not what they were oblig'd to do by the strict Rules of Moral Virtue; for my own part, I declare my self for* Homer *and* Tasso, *and am more in love with* Achilles *and* Rinaldo, *than with* Cyrus *and* Oroondates. *I shall never subject my Characters to the* French *Standard, where Love and Honour are to be weigh'd by Drams and Scruples, yet, where I have design'd the Patterns of exact Virtues, such as in this Play are the Parts of* Almahide, *of* Ozmyn, *and* Benzayda, *I may safely challenge the best of theirs.*

But Almanzor *is tax'd with changing Sides And what Tye has he on him to the contrary? He is not born their Subject whom he serves, and he is injur'd by them to a very high degree. He threatens them, and speaks insolently of Sovereign Power, but so do* Achilles *and* Rinaldo, *who were Subjects and Soldiers to* Agamemnon *and* Godfrey *of* Bulloigne *He talks extravagantly in his Passion, but, if I would take the Pains to quote an hundred Passages of* Ben. Johnson's Cethegus, *I could easily shew you, that the Rhodomontades of* Almanzor *are neither so irrational as his, nor so impossible to be put in execution; for* Cethegus *threatens to destroy Nature, and to raise a new one out of it, to kill all the Senate for*
his

his part of the *Action*; to look *Cato* dead; and a thousand other things as extravagant he says, but performs not one *Action* in the Play.

But none of the former *Calumnies* will stick; and therefore 'tis at last charg'd upon me, that *Almanzor* does all things; or if you will have an absurd *Accusation*, in their *Nonsence* who make it, that he performs Impossibilities; they say, that being a *Stranger*, he appeases two fighting *Factions*, when the *Authority* of their lawful *Soveraign* could not This is indeed the most improbable of all his *Actions*, but 'tis far from being impossible. Their *King* had made himself contemptible to his People, as the *History* of *Granada* tells us; and *Almanzor*, though a *Stranger*, yet was already known to them by his *Gallantry* in the *Juego de toros*, his *Engagement* on the weaker Side, and more especially by the *Character* of his *Person* and brave *Actions*, given by *Abdalla* just before; and after all, the *Greatness* of the *Enterprize* consisted only in the *Daring*, for he had the *King's Guards* to second him But we have read both of *Cæsar*, and many other *Generals*, who have not only calm'd a *Mutiny* with a *Word*, but have presented themselves single before an *Army* of their *Enemies*; which upon sight of them has revolted from their own *Leaders*, and come over to their *Trenches*. In the rest of *Almanzor's Actions* you see him for the most part victorious, but the same *Fortune* has constantly attended many *Heroes* who were not imaginary Yet, you see it no *Inheritance* to him; for, in the *First Part*, he is made a *Prisoner*; and, in the *Last*, defeated, and not able to preserve the *City* from being taken. If the *History* of the late *Duke* of *Guise* be true, he hazarded more, and perform'd not less in *Naples*, than *Almanzor* is feign'd to have done in *Granada*.

I have been too tedious in this *Apology*; but to make some *Satisfaction*, I will leave the rest of my *Play* expos'd to the *Criticks*, without *Defence*

The *Concernment* of it is wholly pass'd from me, and ought to be in them who have been favourable to it, and are somewhat oblig'd to defend their *Opinions*. That there are *Errors* in it, I deny not.

Ast opere in tanto fas est obrepere Somnum.

But I have already swept the *Stakes*, and, with the common good *Fortune* of prosperous *Gamesters*, can be content to sit quietly; to hear my *Fortune* curs'd by some, and my *Faults* arraign'd by others; and to suffer both without *Reply*.

On Mr. DRYDEN's PLAY,

The Conquest of GRANADA.

TH' Applause I gave among the foolish Croud
    Was not distinguish'd, tho' I clapp'd aloud·
Or, if it had, my Judgment had been hid:
I clapp'd for Company, as others did
Thence may be told the Fortune of your Play;
Its Goodness must be try'd another way
Let's judge it then, and, if we've any Skill,
Commend what's good, though we commend it ill.
There will be Praise enough; yet not so much,
As if the World had never any such·
Ben Johnson, Beaumont, Fletcher, Shakespear, are,
As well as you, to have a Poet's Share.
You, who write after, have besides this Curse,
You must write better, or you else write worse.
To equal only what was writ before,
Seems stoll'n, or borrow'd from the former Store.
Though blind as *Homer* all the Ancients be,
'Tis on their Shoulders, like the Lame, we see.
Then not to flatter th' Age, nor flatter you,
(Praises, though less, are greater when they're true)
You're equal to the best, out-done by you;
Who had out-done themselves, had they liv'd now.

VAUGHAN.

PRO-

PROLOGUE

To the First PART.

Spoken by Mrs. *Ellen Gwyn,* in a Broad-brimm'd
Hat and Wafte-Belt.

THIS *Jeft was firft of th' other Houfe's making,*
   And, five times try'd, has never fail'd of taking.
For 'twere a Shame a Poet fhould be kill'd
Under the Shelter of fo broad a Shield.
This is that Hat, whofe very fight did win ye
To laugh and clap as though the Devil were in ye.
As then, for Nokes, fo now I hope you'll be
So dull, to laugh once more for love of me.
I'll write a Play, fays one, for I have got
A Broad-brimm'd Hat, and Wafte-Belt, towards a Plot.
Says th' other, I have one more large than that.
Thus they out-write each other with a Hat.
The Brims ftill grew with ev'ry Play they writ,
And grew fo large, they cover'd all the Wit.
Hat was the Play; 'twas Language, Wit and Tale:
Like them that find Meat, Drink, and Cloth in Ale.
What Dulnefs do thefe Mungril Wits confefs,
When all their Hope is acting of a Drefs!
Thus, Two the beft Comedians of the Age
Muft be worn out, with being Blocks o' th' Stage;

                                             Like

Like a young Girl, who better things has known,
Beneath their Poets Impotence they groan.
See now what Charity it was to save!
They thought you lik'd what only you forgave:
And brought you more dull Senfe, dull Senfe much worfe
Than brisk gay Non-fenfe, and the heavier Curfe.
They bring old Ir'n and Glafs upon the Stage,
To barter with the Indians of our-Age.
Still they write on, and like great Authors show:
But 'tis as Rollers in wet Gardens grow
Heavy with Dirt, and gathering as they go.
May none who have fo little underftood,
To like fuch Trafh, prefume to praife what's good!
And may thofe Drudges of the Stage, whofe Fate
Is damn'd dull Farce, more dully to Tranflate,
Fall under that Excize the State thinks fit
To fet on all French Wares, whofe worft is Wit.
French Farce, worn out at home, is fent abroad;
And patch'd up here, is made our Englifh Mode.
Henceforth let Poets, e'er allow'd to write,
Be fearch'd, like Duelifts before they fight,
For Wheel-broad Hats, dull Humour, all that Chaff,
Which makes you mourn, and makes the Vulgar laugh:
For thefe, in Plays, are as unlawful Arms,
As, in a Combat, Coats of Mail, and Charms.

Persons Represented.

Mahomet Boabdelin, the last King of Granada. — Mr. Kynaston.

Prince Abdalla, his Brother. — Mr Lydal.

Abdelmelech, chief of the Abencerrages. — Mr. Mohun.

Zulema, chief of the Zegrys. — Mr. Harris.

Abenamar, an old Abencerrago. — Mr. Cartwright.

Selin, an old Zegry. — Mr. Wintershal.

Ozmyn, a brave young Abencerrago, Son to Abenamar. — Mr. Beeston.

Hamet, Brother to Zulema, a Zegry. — Mr. Watson.

Gomel, a Zegry. — Mr. Powell.

Almanzor. — Mr. Hart.

Ferdinand, King of Spain. — Mr. Littlewood.

Duke of Arcos, his General. — Mr. Bell.

Don Alonzo d'Aguilar, a Spanish Captain.

Almahide, Queen of Granada. — Mrs. Ellen Guyn.

Lyndaraxa, Sister to Zulema, a Zegry Lady. — Mrs. Marshal.

Benzayda, Daughter to Selin. — Mrs. Boutel.

Esperanza, Slave to the Queen. — Mrs. Reeve.

Halyma, Slave to Lyndaraxa. — Mrs. Eastland.

Isabella, Queen of Spain. — Mrs. James.

Messengers, Guards, Attendants, Men and Women.

The Scene in GRANADA, and the Christian Camp Besieging it.

Alman-

Almanzor and *Almahide*:

OR, THE

CONQUEST

OF

GRANADA.

The First PART.

Boabdelin, Abenamar, Abdelmelech, *Guards.*

Boab. THUS, in the Triumphs of foft Peace, I reign;
 And, from my Walls, defie the Pow'rs of *Spain*;
 With Pomp and Sports my Love I celebrate,
 While they keep diftance, and attend my State.
Parent to her whofe Eyes my Soul enthral;   [*To Aben.*
Whom I, in hope, already Father call;
Abenamar, thy Youth thefe Sports has known,
Of which thy Age is now Spectator grown:
Judge-like thou fit'ft, to praife, or to arraign
The flying Skirmifh of the darted Cane:
But, when fierce Bulls run loofe upon the Place,
And our bold *Moors* their Loves with Danger grace.
Then Heat new bends thy flacken'd Nerves again,
And a fhort Youth runs warm through ev'ry Vein.
 Aben. I muft confefs th' Encounters of this Day
Warm'd me indeed, but quite another way:
Not with the Fire of Youth; but gen'rous Rage,
To fee the Glories of my youthful Age
So far out-done.
 Abdelm. Caftile could never boaft, in all its Pride,
A Pomp fo fplendid; when the Lifts fet wide,
Gave room to the fierce Bulls, which wildly ran
In *Sierra Ronda,* e'er the War began:

Who,

Who, with high Noſtrils, ſnuffling up the Wind,
Now ſtood the Champion of the Salvage kind,
Juſt oppoſite, within the circled Place,
Ten of our bold *Abencerrages* Race
(Each Brandiſhing his Bull-ſpear in his Hand)
Did their proud Gennets gracefully command.
On their ſteel'd Heads their Demy-Lances wore
Small Pennons, which their Ladies Colours bore.
Before this Troop did Warlike *Ozmyn* go;
Each Lady as he rode ſaluting low;
At the chief Stands, with Rev'rence more profound,
His well-taught Courſer, kneeling, touch'd the Ground;
Thence rais'd, he ſidelong bore his Rider on,
Still facing, 'till he out of ſight was gone.
   Boab. You praiſe him like a Friend, and I confeſs
His brave Deportment merited no leſs.
   Abdelm. Nine Bulls were launch'd by his Victorious Arm,
Whoſe wary Gennet ſhunning ſtill the Harm,
Seem'd to attend the Shock, and then leap'd wider
Mean while, his dextrous Rider, when he ſpy'd
The Beaſt juſt ſtooping, 'twixt the Neck and Head
His Lance, with never erring Fury, ſped.
   Aben. My Son did well, and ſo did *Hamet* too;
Yet did no more than we were wont to do;
But what the Stranger did, was more than Man.
   Abdelm. He finiſh'd all thoſe Triumphs we began.
One Bull, with curl'd black Head beyond the reſt,
And Dew-laps hanging from his brawny Cheſt,
With nodding Front a while did daring ſtand,
And with his jetty Hoof ſpurn'd back the Sand:
Then, leaping forth, he bellow'd out aloud:
Th' amaz'd Aſſiſtants back each other croud,
While Monarch-like he rang'd the liſted Field;
Some toſs'd, ſome goar'd, ſome trampling down he kill'd.
Th' ignobler *Moors*, from far his Rage provoke,
With Woods of Darts, which from his Sides he ſhook.
Mean time your Valiant Son, who had before
Gain'd Fame, rode round to ev'ry Mirador;
Beneath each Lady's Stand a ſtop he made,
And, bowing, took th' Applauſes which they paid.
Juſt in that Point of Time the brave Unknown
Approach'd the Liſts.
   Boab. —————————I mark'd him, when alone
(Obſerv'd by all, himſelf obſerving none)
He enter'd firſt; and with a graceful Pride
His fiery *Arab* dext'rouſly did guide:

Who.

Who, while his Rider ev'ry Stand survey'd,
Sprung loose, and flew into an Escapade:
Not moving forward, yet, with ev'ry Bound,
Pressing and seeming still to quit his Ground.
What after pass'd————————
Was far from the *Ventanna* where I sate,
But you were near, and can the Truth relate.   [*To* Abdelm.

    Abdelm. Thus while he stood, the Bull, who saw his Foe,
His easier Conquests proudly did forego:
And, making at him, with a furious Bound,
From his bent Forehead aim'd a double Wound.
A rising Murmur ran through all the Field,
And ev'ry Lady's Blood with Fear was chill'd.
Some shriek'd, while others, with more helpful Care,
Cry'd out aloud, Beware, brave Youth, beware!
At this he turn'd, and as the Bull drew near,
Shunn'd, and receiv'd him on his pointed Spear.
The Lance broke short, the Beast then bellow'd loud,
And his strong Neck to a new Onset bow'd.
Th' undaunted Youth————————
Then drew; and from his Saddle bending low,
Just where the Neck did to the Shoulders grow,
With his full Force discharg'd a deadly Blow.
Not Heads of Poppies (when they reap the Grain)
Fall with more ease before the lab'ring Swain,
Than fell this Head:————————————
It fell so quick, it did even Death prevent:
And made imperfect Bellowings as it went.
Then all the Trumpets Victory did sound:
And yet their Clangors in our Shouts were drown'd.
                                    [*A confus'd Noise within.*

    Boab. Th' Alarm-Bell rings from our *Alhambra* Walls,
And, from the Streets, sound Drums and Ataballes;
                        [*Within, a Bell, Drums and Trumpets.*
How now! from whence proceed these new Alarms?
                                    [*To them a Messenger.*

    Mess. The two fierce Factions are again in Arms:
And, changing into Blood the Day's Delight,
The *Zegrys* with th' *Abencerrages* fight;
On each side their Allies and Friends appear:
The *Macas* here, the *Alabezes* there:
The *Gazuls* with the *Bencerrages* join,
And, with the *Zegrys,* all great *Gomel*'s Line.
    Boab. Draw up behind the *Vivarambla* Place;
Double my Guards, these Factions I will face;

                                                    And

And try if all the Fury they can bring
Be Proof against the Presence of their King.   [*Exit* Boabdelin.
            The Factions appear: At the Head of the Abencerrages,
            Ozmyn; *at the Head of the* Zegrys, Zulema, Hamet,
            Gomel, *and* Selin: *Abenamat and* Abdelmelech *join-
            ed with the* Abencerrages.

Zulema. The faint *Abencerrages* quit their Ground:
Press 'em; put home your Thrusts to ev'ry Wound.

Abdelmelech. Zegry, on Manly Force our Line relies;
Thine poorly takes th' Advantage of Surprize:
Unarm'd and much out-number'd we retreat;
You gain no Fame, when basely you defeat.
If thou art brave seek nobler Victory;
Save *Moorish* Blood; and, while our Bands stand by,
Let two to two an equal Combat try.

Hamet. 'Tis not for Fear the Combat we refuse,
But we our gain'd Advantage will not lose.

Zul. In Combating but two of you will fall;
And we resolve we will dispatch you all.

Ozmyn. We'll double yet th' Exchange before we die,
And each of ours two Lives of yours shall buy.
        Almanzor enters betwixt them, as they stand ready to engage.
    Almanz. I cannot stay to ask which Cause is best;
But this is so to me, because opprest.   [*Goes to the* Abencerrages.
        To them Boabdelin *and his Guards going betwixt them.*
    Boab. On your Allegiance I command you stay;
Who passes here, through me must make his Way.
My Life's the *Isthmos*; through this narrow Line
You first must cut, before those Seas can join.
What Fury, *Zegrys*, has possess'd your Minds?
What Rage the brave *Abencerrages* blinds?
If of your Courage you new Proofs would show,
Without much Travel you may find a Foe.
Those Foes are neither so remote nor few,
That you should need each other to pursue.
Lean Times and foreign Wars should Minds unite;
When poor, Men mutter, but they seldom fight.
O holy *Alha!* that I live to see
Thy *Granadines* assist their Enemy.
You fight the Christians Battels, ev'ry Life
You lavish thus, in this intestine Strife,
Does from our weak Foundations take one Prop,
Which help'd to hold our sinking Country up.

    Ozm. 'Tis fit our private Enmity should cease;
Though injur'd first, yet I will first seek Peace.

                                                Zul.

Zul. No, Murd'rer, no; I never will be won
To Peace with him whose Hand has slain my Son.

Ozm. Our Prophet's Curse————
On me, and all th' *Abencerrages* light,
If unprovok'd I with your Son did fight.

Abdelm. A Band of *Zegrys* ran within the Place,
Match'd with a Troop of Thirty of our Race.
Your Son and *Ozmyn* the first Squadrons led,
Which, ten by ten, like *Parthians* charg'd and fled.
The Ground was strow'd with Canes where we did meet,
Which crackl'd underneath our Coursers Feet:
When *Tarifa* (I saw him ride a-part)
Chang'd his blunt Cane for a Steel-pointed Dart,
And meeting *Ozmyn* next,
Who wanting Time for Treason to provide,
He basely threw it at him, undefy'd.

[*Ozmyn showing his Arm.*

Witness this Blood————which, when by Treason sought,
That follow'd, Sir, which to my self I ought.

Zul. His Hate to thee was grounded on a Grudge
Which all our generous *Zegrys* just did judge:
Thy Villain-Blood thou openly didst place
Above the Purple of our Kingly Race.

Boab. From equal Stems their Blood both Houses draw;
They from *Morocco*, you from *Cordova.*

Hamet. Their Mungril Race is mix'd with Christian Breed,
Hence 'tis that they those Dogs in Prisons feed.

Abdelm. Our Holy Prophet wills, that Charity
Should ev'n to Birds and Beasts extended be:
None knows what Fate is for himself design'd;
The Thought of Human Chance should make us kind.

Gomel. We waste that Time we to Revenge should give:
Fall on, let no *Abencerrago* live. [*Advancing before the rest of his Party.*

[*Almanzor, advancing on the other Side,*
and describing a Line with his Sword.

Upon thy Life pass not this middle Space,
Sure Death stands guarding the forbidden Place.

Gomel. To dare that Death, I will approach yet nigher;
Thus, wert thou compass'd in with circling Fire. [*They fight,*

Boab. Disarm 'em both; if they resist you, kill.

[*Almanzor in the midst of the Guards*
kills Gomel, and then is disarm'd.

Almanz. Now you have but the Leavings of my Will.

Boab. Kill him, this insolent Unknown shall fall,
And be the Victim to attone you all.

That

Ozm. If he must die, not one of us will live;
That Life he gave for us, for him we give.

Boab. It was a Traitor's Voice that spoke those Words;
So are you all who do not sheath your Swords.

Zul. Outrage unpunish'd when a Prince is by,
Forfeits to Scorn the Rights of Majesty.
No Subject his Protection can expect,
Who what he ows himself does first neglect.

Aben. This Stranger, Sir, is he
Who lately in the *Vivarambla* Place
Did, with so loud Applause, your Triumphs grace.

Boab. The Word which I have giv'n I'll not revoke;
If he be brave he's ready for the Stroke.

Almanz. No Man has more Contempt than I of Breath,
But whence hast thou the Right to give me Death?
Obey'd as Sov'raign by thy Subjects be,
But know, that I alone am King of me.
I am as free as Nature first made Man,
E'er the base Laws of Servitude began,
When wild in Woods the noble Savage ran.

Boab. Since then no Pow'r above your own you know,
Mankind should use you like a common Foe,
You should be hunted like a Beast of Prey;
By your own Law I take your Life away.

Almanz. My Laws are made but only for my sake;
No King against himself a Law can make.
If thou pretend'st to be a Prince like me,
Blame not an Act which should thy Pattern be.
I saw th'oppress'd, and thought it did belong
To a King's Office to redress the wrong:
I brought that Succour which thou ought'st to bring,
And so, in Nature, am thy Subjects King.

Boab. I do not want your Counsel to direct,
Or Aid to help me punish or protect.

Almanz. Thou want'st 'em both, or better thou would'st know,
Than to let Factions in thy Kingdom grow.
Divided Int'rests, while thou think'st to sway,
Draw, like two Brooks, thy middle Stream away.
For tho' they band and jar, yet both combine
To make their Greatness by the Fall of thine.
Thus, like a Buckler, thou art held in Sight,
While they, behind thee, with each other fight.

Boab. Away, and execute him instantly.   [*To his Guards.*

Almanz. Stand off; I have not leisure yet to die.
                                    [*To them* Abdalla *hastily.*

Abdal. Hold, Sir, for Heav'n sake hold:

Defer

Defer this noble Stranger's Punishment,
Or your rash Orders you will soon repent.

Boab. Brother, you know not yet his Insolence.

Abdal. Upon your self you punish his Offence:
If we treat gallant Strangers in this sort,
Mankind will shun th'inhospitable Court.
And who, henceforth, to our Defence will come,
If Death must be the brave *Almanzor's* Doom?
From *Africa* I drew him to your Aid;
And for his Succour have his Life betray'd.

Boab. Is this th' *Almanzor* whom at *Fez* you knew,
When first their Swords the *Xeriff* Brothers drew?

Abdal. This, Sir, is he who for the Elder fought,
And to the juster Cause the Conquest brought:
'Till the proud *Santo,* seated in the Throne,
Disdain'd the Service he had done to own.
Then, to the vanquish'd Part his Fate he led;
The Vanquish'd triumph'd, and the Victor fled.
Vast is his Courage, boundless is his Mind,
Rough as a Storm, and humorous as Wind;
Honour's the only Idol of his Eyes:
The Charms of Beauty like a Pest he flies:
And rais'd by Valour, from a Birth unknown,
Acknowledges no Pow'r above his own.

[*Boabdelin coming to* Almanzor.

Impute your Danger to our Ignorance,
The bravest Men are subject most to Chance:
Granada much does to your Kindness owe:
But Towns expecting Sieges, cannot show
More Honour, than t'invite you to a Foe.

Almanz. I do not doubt but I have been to blame:
But, to pursue the End for which I came,
Unite your Subjects first; then let us go,
And pour their common Rage upon the Foe.

Boab. to the Factions.] Lay down your Arms, and let me beg you cease
Your Enmities.

Zul. ————We will not hear of Peace,
'Till we by Force have first reveng'd our slain.

Abdelm. The Action we have done we will maintain.

Selin. Then let the King depart, and we will try
Our Cause by Arms.

Zul. ——————For us and Victory.

Boab. A King intreats you.

Almanz. What Subjects will precarious Kings regard?
A Beggar speaks too softly to be heard.

Lay

Lay down your Arms; 'tis I command you now.
Do it——or, by our Prophet's Soul I vow,
My Hands shall right your King on him I seize.
Now let me see whose Look but disobeys.

Omnes. Long live King *Mahomet Boabdelin.*

Almanz. No more; but hush'd as Midnight Silence go:
He will not have your Acclamations now.
Hence, you unthinking Crowd.——————

[*The common People go off on both Parties.*

Empire, thou poor and despicable thing,
When such as these make or unmake a King!

Abdal. How much of Virtue lyes in one great Soul!

[*Embracing him.*

Whose single Force can Multitudes control!
[*A Trumpet within.*

Enter a Messenger.

Messen. The Duke of *Arcos,* Sir,——
Does with a Trumpet from the Foe appear.

Boab. Attend him, he shall have his Audience here.

Enter the Duke of Arcos.

D. Arcos. The Monarchs of *Castile* and *Arragon*
Have sent me to you, to demand this Town;
To which their just and rightful Claim is known.

Boab. Tell *Ferdinand,* my Right to it appears
By long Possession of eight hundred Years.
When first my Ancestors from *Africk* sail'd,
In *Rodrique's* Death your *Gothick* Title fail'd.

D. Arcos. The Successors of *Rodrique* still remain;
And ever since have held some Part of *Spain.*
Ev'n in the midst of your victorious Pow'rs
Th' *Asturia's,* and all *Portugal* were ours.
You have no Right, except you Force allow;
And if yours then was just, so ours is now.

Boab. 'Tis true; from Force the noblest Title springs;
I therefore hold from that, which first made Kings.

D. Arcos. Since then by Force you prove your Title true,
Ours must be just, because we claim from you.
When with your Father you did jointly reign,
Invading with your *Moors* the South of *Spain,*
I, who that Day the Christians did command,
Then took, and brought you bound to *Ferdinand.*

Boab. I'll hear no more; defer what you would say:
In private we'll discourse some other Day.

D. Arcos. Sir, you shall hear, however you are loth,
That, like a perjur'd Prince, you broke your Oath.
To gain your Freedom you a Contract sign'd,
By which your Crown you to my King resign'd.

From

From thenceforth as his Vaffal holding it,
And paying Tribute such as he thought fit:
Contracting, when your Father came to die,
To lay aside all Marks of Royalty:
And at *Purchena* privately to live;
Which, in exchange, King *Ferdinand* did give.

  Boab. The Force us'd on me made that Contract void.

  D. *Arcos.* Why have you then its Benefits enjoy'd?
By it you had not only Freedom then,
But since had Aid of Mony and of Men.
And, when *Granada* for your Uncle held,
You were by us restor'd, and he expell'd.
Since that in Peace we let you reap your Grain,
Recall'd our Troops that us'd to beat your Plain;
And more————————

  Almanz. Yes, yes, you did with wond'rous Care
Against his Rebels profecute the War,
While he secure in your Protection slept.
For him you took, but for your self you kept.
Thus, as some fawning Usurer does feed
With present Sums th'unwary Spendthrift's Need;
You sold your Kindness at a boundless rate,
And then o're-paid the Debt from his Estate·
Which, mould'ring piece-meal, in your Hands did fall;
'Till now at last you came to swoop it all.

  D. *Arcos.* The Wrong you do my King I cannot bear;
Whose Kindness you would odiously compare.
Th' Estate was his, which yet, since you deny,
He's now content in his own Wrong to buy.

  Almanz. And he shall buy it dear what his he calls·
We will not give one Stone from out these Walls.

  Boab. Take this for Answer, then————
What e'er your Arms have conquer'd of my Land,
I will, for Peace, resign to *Ferdinand:*
To harder Terms my Mind I cannot bring;
But as I still have liv'd, will die a King.

  D. *Arcos.* Since thus you have resolv'd, henceforth prepare
For all the last Extremities of War.
My King his hope from Heav'n's Affistance draws·

  Almanz. The *Moors* have Heav'n and me t'affist their Cause.
Enter Esperanza.   [Exit Arcos.

  Esper. Fair *Almahide*
(Who did with weeping Eyes these Discords see,
And fears the Omen may unlucky be,)
Prepares a *Zambra* to be danc'd this Night,
In hope soft Pleasures may your Minds unite.

Boab.

Boab. My Miftrefs gently chides the Fault I made:
But tedious Bufinefs has my Love delay'd;
Bufinefs, which dares the Joys of Kings invade.
  Almanz. Firft let us fally out, and meet the Foe:
  Abdal. Led on by you we on to Triumph go.
  Boab. Then, with the Day let War and Tumult ceafe·
The Night be facred to our Love and Peace:
'Tis juft fome Joys on weary Kings fhould wait;
'Tis all we gain by being Slaves to State.   *[Exeunt Omnes.*

ACT II.

Abdalla, Abdelmelech, Ozmyn, Zulema, Hamet, *as*
returning from the Sally.

Abdal. THIS happy Day does to *Granada* bring
       A lafting Peace, and Triumphs to the King:
The two fierce Factions will no longer jar,
Since they have now been Brothers in the War:
Thofe, who apart in Emulation fought,
The common Danger to one Body brought;
And to his Coft the proud *Caftilian* finds
Our *Moorifh* Courage in united Minds
  Abdelm. Since to each others Aid our Lives we owe,
Lofe we the Name of Faction and of Foe,
Which I to *Zulema* can bear no more,
Since *Lindaraxa's* Beauty I adore.
  Zul I am oblig'd to *Lindaraxa's* Charms,
Which gain the Conqueft I fhould lofe by Arms;
And wifh my Sifter may continue Fair,
That I may keep a good,
Of whofe Poffeffion I fhould elfe defpair.
  Ozm. While we indulge our common Happinefs,
He is forgot by whom we all poffefs;
The brave *Almanzor*, to whofe Arms we owe
All that we did, and all that we fhall do:
Who, like a Tempeft that out-rides the Wind,
Made a juft Battel e'er the Bodies join'd.
  Abdal. His Victories we fcarce could keep in view,
Or polifh 'em fo faft as he rough-drew.
  Abdelm. Fate, after him, below with Pain did move,
And Victory could fcarce keep Pace above.

Death

Death did at length fo many Slain forget;
And loft the Tale, and took 'em by the great.
[To them Almanzor *with the Duke of Arcos Prifoner.*

Hamet. See here he comes,
And leads in Triumph him who did command
The vanquifh'd Army of King *Ferdinand*
[Almanzor *to the Duke of* Arcos.

Thus far your Mafter's Arms a Fortune find
Below the fwell'd Ambition of his Mind:
And *Alha* fhuts a Mif-believer's Reign
From out the beft and goodlieft part of *Spain.*
Let *Ferdinand Calabrian* Conquefts make,
And from the *French* contefted *Milan* take,
Let him new Worlds difcover to the old,
And break up fhining Mountains big with Gold;
Yet he fhall find this fmall Domeftick Foe,
Still fharp, and pointed, to his Bofom grow;

D. *Arcos.* Of fmall Advantages too much you boaft,
You beat the Out-guards of my Mafter's Hoaft:
This little Lofs, in our vaft Body, fhews
So fmall, that half have never heard the News.
Fame's out of Breath e'er fhe can fly fo far
To tell 'em all, that you have e'er made War.

Almanz. It pleafes me your Army is fo great:
For now I know there's more to Conquer yet
By Heav'n I'll fee what Troops you have behind;
I'll face this Storm that thickens in the Wind:
And, with bent Forehead, full againft it go,
'Till I have found the laft and utmoft Foe.

D *Arcos.* Believe, you fhall not long attend in vain,
To Morrow's Dawn fhall cover all the Plain.
Bright Arms fhall flafh upon you from afar;
A Wood of Lances, and a moving War.
But I, unhappy in my Bands, muft yet
Be only pleas'd to hear of your Defeat:
And, with a Slave's inglorious Eafe remain,
'Till conqu'ring *Ferdinand* has broke my Chain.

Almanz. Vain Man, thy hopes of *Ferdinand* are weak!
I hold thy Chain too faft for him to break.
But fince thou threaten'ft us, I'll fet thee free, —
That I again may fight and conquer thee.

D *Arcos.* Old as I am, I take thee at thy Word,
And will to Morrow thank thee with my Sword.

Almanz. I'll go and inftantly acquaint the King,
And fudden Orders for thy Freedom bring.

Thou

Thou canſt not be ſo pleas'd at Liberty,
As I ſhall be to find thou dar'ſt be free.

[*Exeunt* A!manzor, Arcos, *and the reſt;*
excepting only Abdalla *and* Zulema.

Abdal. Of all thoſe Chriſtians who infeſt this Town,
This Duke of *Arcos* is of moſt Renown.

Zul. Oft have I heard, that in your Father's Reign,
His bold Advent'rers beat the Neighb'ring Plain;
Then, urder *Ponce Leon*'s Name he fought,
And from our Triumphs many Prizes brought.
'Till in Diſgrace from *Spain* at length he went,
And ſince continu'd long in Baniſhment.

Abdal. But ſee, your beauteous Siſter does appear.

[*To them* Lindaraxa.

Zul. By my Deſire ſhe came to find me here

[Zulema *and* Lindaraxa *whiſper; then* Zulema
goes out, and Lindaraxa *is going after.*

Abdal. Why, faireſt *Lindaraxa*, do you fly   [*Staying her.*
A Prince, who at your Feet is proud to die?

Lindaraxa. Sir, I ſhould bluſh to own ſo rude a thing,   [*Staying.*
As 'tis to ſhun the Brother of my King.

Abdal. In my hard Fortune I ſome Eaſe ſhould find,
Did your Diſdain extend to all Mankind.
But give me leave to grieve, and to complain,
That you give others what I beg in vain.

Lindar. Take my Eſteem, if you on that can live,
For, frankly, Sir, 'tis all I have to give.
If, from my Heart you ask or hope for more,
I grieve the Place is taken up before.

Abdal. My Rival merits you.
To *Abdelmelech* I will Juſtice do;
For he wants Worth who dares not praiſe a Foe.

Lindar. That for his Virtue, Sir, you make Defence,
Shows in your own a noble Confidence:
But him defending, and excuſing me,
I know not what can your Advantage be.

Abdal. I fain would ask, e'er I proceed in this,
If, as by Choice, you are by Promiſe his?

Lindar. Th'Engagement only in my Love does lye,
But that's a Knot which you can ne'er untie.

Abdal. When Cities are Beſieg'd, and Treat to yield,
If there appear Relievers from the Field,
The Flag of Parley may be taken down,
'Till the Succeſs of thoſe without are known.

Lindar. Though *Abdelmelech* has not yet poſſeſt,
Yet I have ſeal'd the Treaty for my Breaſt.

Abdal.

Abdal. Your Treaty has not ty'd you to a Day;
Some Chance might break it, would you but delay:
If I can judge the Secrets of your Heart,
Ambition in it has the greatest Part;
And Wisdom then will shew some difference,
Betwixt a private Person and a Prince.

Lindar. Princes are Subjects still——
Subject and Subject can small Diff'rence bring:
The Diff'rence is 'twixt Subjects and a King.
And since, Sir, you are none, your Hopes remove;
For less than Empire I'll not change my Love.

Abdal. Had I a Crown, all I should prize in it,
Should be the Pow'r to lay it at your Feet.

Lindar. Had you that Crown, which you but wish, not hope,
Then I, perhaps, might stoop, and take it up.
But 'till your Wishes and your Hopes agree,
You shall be still a private Man with me.

Abdal. If I am King, and if my Brother die——
Lindar. Two If's scarce make one Possibility.
Abdal. The Rule of Happiness by Reason scan;
You may be happy with a private Man.

Lindar. That Happiness I may enjoy, 'tis true,
But then that private Man must not be you.
Where e'er I love, I'm happy in my Choice;
If I make you so, you shall pay my Price.

Abdal. Why would you be so great?
Lindar. ——————Because I've seen,
This Day, what 'tis to hope to be a Queen.
Heav'n, how y'all watch'd each Motion of her Eye!
None could be seen while *Almahide* was by,
Because she is to be Her Majesty.
Why would I be a Queen! because my Face
Would wear the Title with a better Grace.
If I became it not, yet it would be
Part of your Duty, then, to flatter me.
These are but half the Charms of being Great;
I would be somewhat——that I know not yet:
Yes; I avow th' Ambition of my Soul,
To be that One to live without Control:
And that's another Happiness to me,
To be so happy as but one can be.

Abdal. Madam, (because I would all Doubts remove)
Would you, were I a King, accept my Love?

Lindar. I would accept it, and, to show 'tis true,
From any other Man as soon as you.

Abdal.

Abd l Your sharp Replies make me not love you lefs;
But make me feek new Paths to Happinefs.
What I defign, by Time will beft be feen.
You may be mine, and yet may be a Queen:
When you are fo, your Word your Love affures.

    Lada . Perhaps not love yo——but I will be yours.

              [He offers to take her Hand and kifs it.

Stay, Sir, that Grace I cannot yet allow,
Before you fee the Crown upon my Brow.
That Favour which you feek——
Or *Abdelmelech* or a King muft have,
When you are fo, then you may be my Slave.

            [Exit, but looks fmiling back on him.

    Abd . How e'er imperious in her Words fhe were,
Her parting Looks had nothing of Severe.
A glancing Smile allur'd me to command;
And her foft Fingers gently prefs'd my Hand.
I felt the Pleafure glide through ev'ry Part,
Her Hand went through me to my very Heart
For fuch another Pleafure, did he live,
I could my Father of a Crown deprive.
What did I fay!
Father! that impious Thought has fhock'd my Mind
How bold our Paffions are, and yet how blind!
She's gone, and now
Methinks there is lefs Glory in a Crown,
My boyling Paffions fettle and go down
Like Amber chaf'd, when fhe is near fhe acts,
When farther off, inclines, but not attracts.

                              [To him Zulema.

Affift me, *Zulema*, if thou wouldft be
That Friend thou feem'ft, affift me againft me.
Betwixt my Love and Virtue I am tofs'd,
This muft be forfeited, or that be loft
I could do much to merit thy Applaufe,
Help me to fortifie the better Caufe
My Honour is not wholly put to Flight,
But would, if feconded, renew the Sight.

    Zul I met my Sifter, but I do not fee
What Difficulty in your Choice can be
She told me all, and 'tis fo plain a Cafe,
You need not ask what Counfel to embrace.

    Abdal. I ftand reprov'd that I did doubt at all,
My wafting Virtue ftay'd out for thy Call
Tis plain that fhe, who, for a Kingdom, now
Would facrifice her Love, and break her Vow,

                                  Not

Not out of Love but Int'reſt acts alone,
And would, ev'n in my Arms, lye thinking of a Throne.

　Zul. Add to the reſt this one Reflection more,
When ſhe is marry'd, and you ſtill adoie,
Think then, and think what Comfort it will bring,
She had been mine———
Had I but only dar'd to be a King.

　Abdal I hope you only would my Honour try;
I'm loth to think you Virtue's Enemy.

　Zul. If, when a Crown and Miſtreſs are in place,
Virtue intrudes with hei lean holy Face;
Virtue's then mine, and not I Virtue's Foe:
Why does ſhe come where ſhe has nought to do?
Let hei with Anch'iites not with Loveis lye,
States-men and they keep better Company.

　Abdal Reaſon was giv'n to cuib our head-ſtrong Will.

　Zul. Reaſon but ſhews a weak Phyſician's Skill.
Gives nothing while the raging Fit does laſt;
But ſtays to cure it when the worſt is paſt.
Reaſon's a Staff foi Age, when Nature's gone,
But Youth is ſtrong enough to walk alone

　Abdal. In curſs'd Ambition I no Reſt ſhould find;
But muſt for ever loſe my Peace of Mind.

　Zul. Methinks that Peace of Mind were bravely loſt,
A Crown, what e'er we give, is worth the Coſt.

　Abdal. Juſtice diſtributes to each Man his Right,
But what ſhe gives not, ſhould I take by Might?

　Zul. If Juſtice will take all and nothing give,
Juſtice, methinks, is not diſtributive.

　Abdal. Had Fate ſo pleas'd, I had been eldeſt-born,
And then, without a Crime, the Crown had worn.

　Zul Would you ſo pleaſe, Fate yet a way would find;
Man makes his Fate according to his Mind.
The weak low Spirit Fortune makes her Slave,
But ſhe's a Drudge, when hector'd by the Biave.
If Fate weaves common Thread, he'll change the Doom,
And with new Purple ſpiead a nobler Loom.

　Abdal No moie,———I will uſurp the Royal Seat;
Thou, who haſt made me wicked, make me great.

　Zul. Your Way is plain, the Death of *Tarifa*
Does on the King our *Zegrys* Hatred draw
Though with our Enemies in ſhow we cloſe,
'Tis but while we to puipoſe can be Foes.
Selin, who heads us, would revenge his Son,
But Favoui hinders Juſtice to be done,

E　　　　　　　　　Pioud

Proud *Ozmyn* with the King his Pow'r maintains;
And, in him, each *Abencerrago* reigns.

Abdal. What face of any Title can I bring?

Zul. The Right an eldeſt Son has to be King.
Your Father was at firſt a private Man,
And got your Brother e'er his Reign began.
When by his Valour he the Crown had won,
Then you were born, a Monarch's Eldeſt Son.

Abdal. To ſharp-ey'd Reaſon this would ſeem untrue,
But Reaſon I through Love's falſe Opticks view.

Zul. Love's mighty Pow'r has led me Captive too;
I am in it unfortunate as you.

Abdal. Our Loves and Fortunes ſhall together go;
Thou ſhalt be happy when I firſt am ſo.

Zul. The *Zegrys* at old *Selin's* Houſe are met,
Where, in cloſe Council, for Revenge they ſit:
There we our common Int'reſt will unite;
You their Revenge ſhall own, and they your Right.
One thing I had forgot, which may import;
I met *Almanzor* coming back from Court,
But with a diſcompos'd and ſpeedy Pace,
A fiery Colour kindling all his Face:
The King his Priſ'ner's Freedom has deny'd,
And that Refuſal has provok'd his Pride.

Abdal. Would he were ours!
I'll try to gild th' Injuſtice of his Cauſe,
And court his Valour with a vaſt Applauſe.

Zul. The Bold are but the Inſtruments o'th' Wiſe·
They undertake the Dangers we adviſe.
And while our Fabrick with their Pains we raiſe,
We take the Profit, and pay them with Praiſe.   [*Exeunt.*

ACT III.

Almanzor, Abdalla.

Almanz. **T**HAT he ſhould dare to do me this Diſgrace!
Is Fool or Coward writ upon my Face?
Refuſe my Priſ'ner! I ſuch Means will uſe,
He ſhall not have a Priſ'ner to refuſe.

Abdal. He ſaid you were not by your Promiſe ty'd;
That he abſolv'd your Word when he deny'd.

Almanz.

Almanz. He break my Promise, and absolve my Vow!
'Tis more than *Mahomet* himself can do.
The Word which I have giv'n shall stand like Fate;
Not like the King's, that Weather-cock of State.
He stands so high, with so unfix'd a Mind,
Two Factions turn him with each Blast of Wind.
But now he shall not veer; my Word is past:
I'll take his Heart by th' Roots, and hold it fast.

Abdal. You have your Veng'ance in your Hand this Hour,
Make me the humble Creature of your Pow'r:
The *Granadines* will gladly me obey;
(Tir'd with so base and impotent a Sway.)
And when I shew my Title, you shall see
I have a better Right to Reign, than he.

Almanz. It is sufficient that you make the Claim :
You wrong our Friendship when your Right you name.
When for my self I fight, I weigh the Cause;
But Friendship will admit of no such Laws:
That weighs by th' lump, and, when the Cause is light,
Puts Kindness in to set the Ballance right.
True, I would wish my Friend the juster side:
But in th' unjust my Kindness more is try'd.
And all the Opposition I can bring,
Is, that I fear to make you such a King.

Abdal. The Majesty of Kings we should not blame,
When Royal Minds adorn the Royal Name :
The Vulgar, Greatness too much Idolize,
But haughty Subjects it too much despise.

Almanz. I only speak of him,
Whom Pomp and Greatness sit so loose about,
That he wants Majesty to fill them out.

Abdal Haste then, and lose no time———
The Business must be enterpriz'd this Night.
We must surpize the Court in its Delight.

Almanz. For you to Will, for me 'tis to Obey;
But I would give a Crown in open Day:
And, when the *Spaniards* their Assault begin,
At once beat those without, and these within.   [*Exit* Almanzor.
                    Enter Abdelmelech.

Abdelm. *Abdalla,* hold; there's somewhat I intend
To speak, not as your Rival, but your Friend.

Abdal. If as a Friend, I am oblig'd to hear;
And what a Rival says I cannot fear.

Abdelm. Think, brave *Abdalla,* what it is you do:
Your Quiet, Honour, and our Friendship too,
All for a fickle Beauty you forego.

E 2   Think

Think, and turn back, before it be too late;
Behold in me th' Example of your Fate.
I am your Sea-mark, and though wrack'd and loft,
My Ruins ftand to warn you from the Coaft.

   Abdal. Your Councils, noble *Abdelmelech*, move
My Reafon to accept 'em; not my Love.
Ah, why did Heav'n leave Man fo weak Defence,
To truft frail Reafon with the Rule of Senfe!
'Tis over-pois'd, and kick'd up in the Air,
While Senfe weighs down the Scale, and keeps it there.
Or, like a Captive King, 'tis born away;
And forc'd to count'nance its own Rebel's Sway.

   Abdelm. No, no; our Reafon was not vainly lent;
Nor is a Slave, but by its own Confent:
If Reafon on his Subject's Triumph wait,
An eafie King deferves no better Fate.

   Abdal. You fpeak too late; my Empire's loft too far,
I cannot fight.

   Abdelm. ———Then make a flying War;
Diflodge betimes before you are befet.

   Abdal. Her Tears, her Smiles, her ev'ry Look's a Net.
Her Voice is like a Syren's of the Land,
And bloody Hearts lye panting in her Hand.

   Abdelm. This do you know, and tempt the Danger ftill?

   Abdal. Love, like a Lethargy, has feiz'd my Will.
I'm not my felf, fince from her fight I went,
I lean my Trunk that way, and there ftand bent.
As one, who in fome frightful Dream, would fhun
His preffing Foe, labours in vain to run;
And his own Slownefs in his Sleep bemoans,
With thick fhort Sighs, weak Cries, and tender Groans,
So I ————

   Abdelm. ——— Some Friend, in Charity, fhould fhake
And rouze, and call you loudly 'till you wake.
Too well I know her Blandifhments to gain,
Ufurper-like, 'till fettl'd in her Reign;
Then proudly fhe infults, and gives you Cares
And Jealoufies, fhort Hopes, and long Defpairs.
To this hard Yoke you muft hereafter bow;
How e'er fhe fhines all Golden to you now.

   Abdal. Like him, who on the Ice————
Slides fwiftly on, and fees the Water near,
Yet cannot ftop himfelf in his Career:
So am I carry'd. This Enchanted Place,
Like *Circe's* Ifle, is Peopl'd with a Race

Of Dogs and Swine, yet, though their Fate I know,
I look with Pleasure, and am turning too.

                     [*Lyndaraxa passes over the Stage.*

   Abdelm. Fly, fly, before th' Allurements of her Face;
E'er she return with some resistless Grace,
And with new Magick covers all the Place.

   Abdal. I cannot, will not; nay, I would not fly;
I'll love, be blind, be cozen'd 'till I die.
And you, who bid me wiser Counsel take,
I'll hate, and, if I can, I'll kill you for her sake.

   Abdelm. Ev'n I that counsell'd you, that Choice approve;
I'll hate you blindly, and her blindly love:
Prudence, that stemm'd the Stream, is out of Breath,
And to go down it is the easier Death.

     Lyndaraxa *Re-enters, and smiles on* Abdalla.

                     [*Exit* Abdalla.

   Abdelm. That Smile on Prince *Abdalla*, seems to say
You are not in your killing Mood to Day,
Men brand, indeed, your Sex with Cruelty,
But you're too good to see poor Lovers die.
This God-like Pity in you I extol;
And more, because, like Heaven's, 'tis general.

   Lyndar. My Smile implies not that I grant his Suit:
'Twas but a bare Return of his Salute.

   Abdelm. It said, you were engag'd, and I in Place:
But, to please both, you would divide the Grace.

   Lyndar. You've Cause to be contented with your Part,
When he has but the Look, and you the Heart.

   Abdelm. In giving but that Look, you give what's mine:
I'll not one corner of a Glance resign:
All's mine, and I am cov'tous of my Store:
I have not Love enough, I'll tax you more.

   Lyndar. I gave not Love, 'twas but Civility:
He is a Prince; that's due to his Degree.

   Abdelm. That Prince you smil'd on is my Rival still;
And should, if me you lov'd, be treated ill.

   Lyndar. I know not how to show so rude a Spight.

   Abdelm. That is, you know not how to love aright;
Or, if you did, you would more difference see
Betwixt our Souls, than 'twixt our Quality.
Mark, if his Birth makes any difference,
If, to his Words, it adds one grain of Sense:
That Duty which his Birth can make his due
I'll pay, but it shall not be paid by you.
For if a Prince Courts her whom I adore,
He is my Rival, and a Prince no more.

                          Lyndar.

Lyndar. And when did I my Pow'r so far resign,
That you should regulate each Look of mine?

Abdelm. Then, when you gave your Love, you gave that Pow'r.

Lyndar. 'Twas during Pleasure, 'tis revok'd this Hour.
Now call me false, and rail on Womankind,
'Tis all the Remedy you're like to find.

Abdelm. Yes, there's one more,
I'll hate you, and this Visit is my last.

Lyndar. Do't, if you can; you know I hold you fast.
Yet, for your Quiet, would you could resign
Your Love, as easily as I do mine.

Abdelm. Furies and Hell, how unconcern'd she speaks!
With what indifference all her Vows she breaks!
Curse on me; but she smiles.

Lyndar. That Smile's a part of Love; and all's your Due ·
I take it from the Prince, and give it you.

Abdelm. Just Heav'n, must my poor Heart your May-game prove,
To Bandy, and make Children's Play in Love?   [*Half Crying.*
Ah! how have I this Cruelty deserv'd?
I, who so truly and so long have serv'd!
And left so easily! oh cruel Maid!
So easily! 'twas too unkindly said.
That Heart which could so easily remove,
Was never fix'd, nor rooted deep in Love.

Lyndar. You lodg'd it so uneasie in your Breast,
I thought you had been weary of the Guest,
First I was treated like a Stranger there;
But, when a Houshold Friend I did appear,
You thought, it seems, I could not live elsewhere.
Then, by degrees, your feign'd Respect withdrew:
You mark'd my Actions, and my Guardian grew.
But, I am not concern'd your Acts to blame:
My Heart to yours but upon Liking came;
And, like a Bird, whom prying Boys molest,
Stays not to breed, where she had built her Nest.

Abdelm. I have done ill———
And dare not ask you to be less displeas'd:
Be but more angry, and my Pain is eas'd.

Lyndar. If I should be so kind a Fool, to take
This little Satisfaction which you make,
I know you would presume some other time
Upon my Goodness, and repeat your Crime.

Abdelm. Oh never, never, upon no Pretence;
My Life's too short to expiate this Offence.

Lyndar. No, now I think on't, 'tis in vain to try;
'Tis in your Nature, and past Remedy.

You'll

You'll ftill difquiet my too loving Heart:
Now we are Friends 'tis beft for both to part.　　　*Taking her Hand.*

   Abdelm. By this——Will you not give me leave to fwear!

   Lyndar. You would be perjur'd if you fhould, I fear.
And when I talk with Prince *Abdalla* next,
I with your fond Sufpicions fhall be vext.

   Abdelm. I cannot fay I'll conquer Jealoufie;
But, if you'll freely pardon me, I'll try.

   Lyndar. And, 'till you that fubmiffive Servant prove,
I never can conclude you truly love.

To them, the King, Almahide, Abenamar, Efperanza, *Guards, Attendants.*

   King. Approach, my *Almahide,* my charming Fair;
Bleffing of Peace, and Recompence of War.
This Night is yours, and may your Life ftill be
The fame in Joy, though not Solemnity.

The Zambra Dance.

SONG.

1.

Beneath a *Myrtle Shade,*
Which Love for none but happy Lovers made,
I flept; and ftraight my Love before me brought
Phillis, *the Object of my waking Thought:*
Undrefs'd fhe came my Flames to meet,
While Love ftrow'd Flow'rs beneath her Feet;
Flow'rs, which fo prefs'd by her, became more fweet.

2.

From the bright Vifion's Head
A carelefs Veil of Lawn was loofely fpread:
From her white Temples fell her fhaded Hair,
Like cloudy Sun-fhine, not too brown nor fair;
Her Hands, her Lips did Love infpire,
Her ev'ry Grace my Heart did fire:
But moft her Eyes, which languifh'd with Defire.

3.

Ah, charming Fair, faid I,
How long can you my Blifs and yours deny?
By Nature and by Love, this lonely Shade
Was for revenge of fuff'ring Lovers made.
Silence and Shades with Love agree:
Both fhelter you and favour me,
You cannot blufh, becaufe I cannot fee.

4. *No.*

4.

No, let me die, she said,
Rather than lose the spotless Name of Maid:
Faintly, methought, she spoke; for all the while
She bid me not believe her, with a Smile.
Then die, said I: She still deny'd;
And is it thus, thus, thus, she cry'd,
You use a harmless Maid, and so she dy'd!

5.

I wak'd, and straight I knew
I lov'd so well it made my Dream prove true:
Fancy, the kinder Mistress of the two,
Fancy had done what Phillis would not do!
Ah, cruel Nymph, cease your Disdain,
While I can dream you scorn in vain!
Asleep or waking you must ease my Pain.

            [*After the Dance, a tumultuous Noise*
                of Drums and Trumpets.
       To them Ozmyn; *his Sword drawn.*

Ozm. Arm, quickly, arm; yet all, I fear, too late:
The Enemy's already at the Gate.
  Boab. The Christians are dislodg'd; what Foe is near?
  Ozm. The *Zegrys* are in Arms, and almost here.
The Streets with Torches shine, with Shoutings ring,
And Prince *Abdalla* is proclaim'd the King.
What Man could do I have already done,
But bold *Almanzor* fiercely leads 'em on.
  Aben. Th'*Alhambra* yet is safe in my Command,   [*To the King.*
Retreat you thither while their Shock we stand.
  Boab. I cannot meanly for my Life provide;
I'll either perish in't, or stem this Tide.
To guard the Palace, *Ozmyn,* be your Care,
If they o'ercome, no Sword will hurt the Fair.
  Ozm. I'll either die, or I'll make good the Place.
  Abdelm. And I, with these, will bold *Almanzor* face.
          [*Exeunt all but the Ladies. An Alarm within.*
  Almah. What dismal Planet did my Triumphs light?
Discord the Day, and Death does rule the Night:
The Noise my Soul does through my Senses wound.
  Lyndar. Methinks it is a noble, sprightly Sound.
The Trumpet's Clangor, and the Clash of Arms!
This Noise may chill your Blood; but mine it warms:
          [*Shouting and clashing of Swords within.*
We have already pass'd the *Rubicon.*
The Dice are mine; now, Fortune, for a Throne.
         [*A Shout within, and clashing of Swords afar off.*
                    The

The Sound goes farther off, and faintly dies;
Curse of this going back, these ebbing Cries!
Ye Winds, waft hither Sounds more strong and quick;
Beat faster, Drums, and mingle Deaths more thick.
I'll to the Turrets of the Palace go,
And add new Fire to those that fight below:
Thence, Hero-like, with Torches by my side,
(Far be the Omen, tho',) my Love I'll guide.
No; like his better Fortune I'll appear,
With open Arms, loose Veil, and flowing Hair,
Just flying forward from my rolling Sphere:
My Smiles shall make *Abdalla* more than Man;
Let him look up and perish if he can.   [*Exit.*

   An Alarm nearer: Then Enter Almanzor *and* Selin, *in the*
       Head of the Zegrys; Osmyn *Prisoner.*

  Almanz. We have not fought enough; they fly too soon:
And I am griev'd the noble Sport is done.
This only Man, of all whom Chance did bring

                         [*Pointing to* Ozmyn.

To meet my Arms, was worth the Conquering.
His brave Resistance did my Fortune grace;
So slow, so threatning forward he gave Place.
His Chains be easie, and his Usage fair.
  Selin. I beg you would commit him to my Care.
  Almanz. Next, the brave *Spaniard* free without delay;
And with a Convoy send him safe away.   [*Exit a Guard.*

       To them Hamet *and others.*

  Hamet. The King by me salutes you; and, to show
That to your Valour he his Crown does owe,
Would from your Mouth I should the Word receive,
And that to these you would your Orders give.
  Almanz. He much o'er-rates the little I have done.

   [Almanzor *goes to the Door, and there seems to give*
     out Orders, by sending People several Ways.

    Selin to Ozmyn.

Now to revenge the Murder of my Son.
To Morrow for thy certain Death prepare;
This Night I only leave thee to despair.
  Ozmyn. Thy idle Menaces I do not fear:
My Bus'ness was to die or conquer here.
Sister, for you I grieve I could no more;
My present State betrays my want of Pow'r.
But, when true Courage is of Force bereft,
Patience, the only Fortitude, is left.   [*Exit cum* Selin.
  Almah. Ah, *Esperanza,* what for me remains
But Death, or, worse than Death, inglorious Chains!

             F   *Esper.*

Esper. Madam, you must not to Despair give place;
Heav'n never meant Misfortune to that Face.
Suppose there were no Justice in your Cause,
Beauty's a Bribe that gives her Judges Laws.
That you are brought to this deplor'd Estate,
Is but th' ingenious Flattery of your Fate;
Fate fears her Succour, like an Alms, to give,
And would you, God-like, from your self should live.

   Almah. Mark but how terribly his Eyes appear!
And yet there's something roughly noble there,
Which, in unfashion'd Nature, looks Divine;
And like a Gem does in the Quarry shine.

          [*Almanzor returns; she falls at his Feet being veil'd.*

   Almah. Turn, mighty Conqu'ror, turn your Face this way,
Do not refuse to hear the wretched pray.

   Almanz. What business can this Woman have with me?

   Almah. That of th' afflicted to the Deity.
So may your Arms Success in Battels find;
So may the Mistress of your Vows be kind,
If you have any; or, if you have none,
So may your Liberty be still your own.

   Almanz. Yes, I will turn my Face, but not my Mind;
You Bane and soft Destruction of Mankind,
What would you have with me?

   Almah. —————I beg the grace   [*Unveiling.*
You would lay by those Terrors of your Face.
'Till Calmness to your Eyes you first restore,
I am afraid, and I can beg no more.

    Almanz. *looking fixedly on her.*
   Well; my fierce Visage shall not murder you·
Speak quickly, Woman; I have much to do.

   Almah. Where should I find the Heart to speak one Word?
Your Voice, Sir, is as killing as your Sword.
As you have left the Lightning of your Eye,
So would you please to lay your Thunder by.

   Almanz. I'm pleas'd and pain'd, since first her Eyes I saw,
As I were stung with some *Tarantula:*
Arms and the dusty Field I less admire,
And soften strangely in some new Desire.
Honour burns in me not so fiercely bright,
But pale, as Fires when master'd by the Light.
Ev'n while I speak and look, I change yet more;
And now am nothing that I was before.
I'm mumm'd, and fix'd, and scarce my Eye-balls move;
I fear it is the Lethary of Love!

'Tis he; I feel him now in ev'ry Part:
Like a new Lord he vaunts about my Heart,
Surveys in State each corner of my Breaft,
While poor fierce I, that was, am difpoffeft.
I'm bound, but I will rouze my Rage again:
And though no hope of Liberty remain,
I'll fright my Keeper when I fhake my Chain.
You are————   [*Angerly.*

   Almah. ——— I know I am your Captive, Sir.

   Almanz. You are——You fhall——And I can fcarce forbear——

   Almah. Alas!

   Almanz. 'Tis all in vain; it will not do: [*Afide.*
I cannot now a feeming Anger fhow:
My Tongue againft my Heart no Aid affords,
For Love ftill rifes up, and choaks my Words.

   Almah. In half this time a Tempeft would be ftill.

   Almanz. 'Tis you have rais'd that Tempeft in my Will.
I wo'not love you, give me back my Heart;
But give it as you had it, fierce and brave;
It was not made to be a Woman's Slave:
But, Lion-like, has been in Defarts bred;
And, us'd to range, will ne'er be tamely led.
Reftore its Freedom to my fetter'd Will,
And then I fhall have Pow'r to ufe you ill.

   Almah. My fad Condition may your Pity move;
But look not on me with the Eyes of Love.———
I muft be brief, though I have much to fay.

   Almanz. No, fpeak; for I can hear you now, all Day:
Her fuing fooths me with a fecret Pride: [*Softly.*
A fuppliant Beauty cannot be deny'd: [*Afide.*
Ev'n while I frown, her Charms the Furrows feize;
And I'm corrupted with the Pow'r to pleafe.

   Almah. Though in your worth no Caufe of Fear I fee;
I fear the Infolence of Victory:
As you are Noble, Sir, protect me then,
From the rude Outrage of infulting Men.

   Almanz. Who dares touch her I love? I'm all o'er Love:
Nay, I am Love; Love fhot, and fhot fo faft,
He fhot himfelf into my Breaft at laft.

   Almah. You fee before you her who fhould be Queen,
Since fhe is promis'd to *Boabdelin.*

   Almanz. Are you belov'd by him? O wretched Fate,
Firft that I love at all; then, lov'd too late!
Yet, I muft love!

   Almah. ———————Alas, it is in vain;
Fate for each other did not us ordain.

The

The Chances of this Day too clearly show
That Heav'n took Care that it should not be so.

   Almanz. Would Heav'n had quite forgot me this one Day,
But Fate's yet hot———————
I'll make it take a bent another way.
                  [He walks swiftly and discomposedly, studying.
I bring a Claim which does his Right remove:
You're his by Promise, but you're mine by Love.
'Tis all but Ceremony which is past:
The Knot's to tie which is to make you fast.
Fate gave not to *Boabdelin* that Pow'r:
He Woo'd you but as my Ambassador.

   Almah. Our Souls are ty'd by Holy Vows above.

   Almanz. He sign'd but his; but I will seal my Love.
I love you better; with more Zeal than he.

   Almah. This Day———————
I gave my Faith to him, he his to me.

   Almanz. Good Heav'n, thy Book of Fate before me lay,
But to tear out the Journal of this Day.
Or, if the Order of the World below
Will not the Gap of one whole Day allow,
Give me that Minute when she made her Vow.
" That Minute, ev'n the happy from their Bliss might give,
" And those who live in Grief a shorter time would live.
So small a Link, if broke, th' Eternal Chain
Would, like divided Waters, join again.
It wo'not be; the Fugitive is gone;
Prest by the Crowd of following Minutes on:
That precious Moment's out of Nature fled,
And in the Heap of common Rubbish laid,
Of things that once have been, and are decay'd.

   Almah. Your Passion, like a Fright, suspends my Pain:
It meets, o'er-pow'rs, and beats mine back again:
But, as when Tides against the Current flow,
The Native Stream runs its own Course below:
So, though your Griefs possess the upper Part,
My own have deeper Channels in my Heart.

   Almanz. Forgive that Fury which my Soul does move,
'Tis the Essay of an untaught first Love.   *an untaught first love*
Yet rude, unfashion'd Truth it does express:
'Tis Love just peeping in a hasty Dress.
Retire, Fair Creature, to your needful Rest;
There's something Noble lab'ring in my Breast:
This raging Fire, which through the Mass does move,
Shall purge my Dross, and shall refine my Love.
                [Exeunt Almahide *and* Esperanza.
                        She

She goes, and I like my own Ghoft appear;
It is not living, when fhe is not here.

[*To him* Abdalla *as King,* attended.

Abdal. My firft Acknowledgments to Heav'n are due:
My next, *Almanzor,* let me pay to you.

Almanz. A poor Surprize, and on a naked Foe.
What ever you confefs, is all you owe.
And I no Merit own, or underftand
That Fortune did you Juftice by my Hand.
Yet, if you will that little Service pay
With a great Favour, I can fhew the way.

Abdal. I have a Favour to demand of you;
That is, to take the thing for which you fue.

Almanz. Then, briefly, thus; when I th' *Albayzyn* won,
I found the beauteous *Almahide* alone:
Whofe fad Condition did my Pity move:
And that Compaffion did produce my Love.

Abdal. This needs no Suit; in Juftice, I declare,
She is your Captive by the Right of War.

Almanz. She is no Captive then; I fet her free:
And, rather than I will her Jailor be,
I'll nobly lofe her in her Liberty.

Abdal. Your Generofity I much approve,
But your excefs of that fhows want of Love.

Almanz. No, 'tis th' excefs of Love, which mounts fo high,
That, feen far off, it leffens to the Eye.
Had I not lov'd her, and had fet her free,
That, Sir, had been my Generofity:
But 'tis exalted Paffion, when I fhow
I dare be wreched, not to make her fo.
And, while another Paffion fills her Breaft,
I'll be all wretched rather than half bleft.

Abdal. May your Heroick Act fo profperous be,
That *Almahide* may figh you fet her free.

Enter Zulema.

Zul. Of Five tall Tow'rs which fortifie this Town,
All but th' *Alhambra* your Dominion own.
Now therefore boldly I confefs a Flame,
Which is excus'd in *Almahide's* Name.
If you the Merit of this Night regard,
In her Poffeffion I have my Reward.

Almanz. She your Reward! why, fhe's a Gift fo great——
That I my felf have not deferv'd her yet.
And therefore, though I won her with my Sword,
I have, with awe, my Sacrilege reftor'd.

Zul. What you deserve————
I'll not difpute, becaufe I do not know,
This only I will fay, She fhall not go.

Almanz. Thou, fingle, art not worth my anfwering,
But take what Friends, what Armies thou canft bring;
What Worlds, and when you are united all,
Then, I will thunder in your Ears.————She fhall.

Zul. I'll not one Tittle of my Right refign;
Sir, your implicite Promife made her mine.
When I in general Terms my Love did fhow,
You fwore our Fortunes fhould together go.

Abdal. The Merits of the Caufe I'll not decide,
But, like my Love, I would my Gift divide,
Your equal Titles then no longer plead;
But one of you for love of me recede.

Almanz. I have receded to the utmoft Line,
When, by my free Confent, fhe is not mine.
Then let him equally recede with me,
And both of us will join to fet her free.

Zul. If you will free your part of her you may;
But, Sir, I love not your Romantick way.
Dream on; enjoy her Soul, and fet that free;
I'm pleas'd her Perfon fhould be left for me.

Almanz. Thou fhalt not wifh her thine; thou fhalt not dare
To be fo impudent, as to defpair.

Zul. The *Zegrys*, Sir, are all concern'd to fee
How much their Merit you neglect in me.

Hamet. Your flighting *Zulema*, this very Hour
Will take ten thoufand Subjects from your Pow'r.

Almanz. What are ten thoufand Subjects fuch as they?
If I am fcorn'd————I'll take my felf away.

Abdal. Since both cannot poffefs what both purfue;
I grieve, my Friend, the Chance fhould fall on you.
But when you hear what Reafons I can urge————

Almanz. None, none that your Ingratitude can purge.
Reafon's a Trick, when it no Grant affords:
It ftamps the Face of Majefty on Words.

Abdal. Your Boldnefs to your Services I give:
Now take it as your full Reward to live.

Almanz. To live!
If from my Hands alone my Death can be,
I am Immortal, and a God to thee.
If I would kill thee now, thy Fate's fo low
That I muft ftoop e'er I can give the Blow.
But mine is fix'd fo far above thy Crown,

That all thy Men,
Pil'd on thy Back, can never pull it down.
But at my Eafe thy Deftiny I fend,
By ceafing from this Hour to be thy Friend.
Like Heav'n, I need but only to ftand ftill;
And, not concurring to thy Life, I kill.
Thou canft no Title to my Duty bring;
I'm not thy Subject, and my Soul's thy King.
Farewel: When I am gone
There's not a Star of thine dare ftay with thee:
I'll whiftle thy tame Fortune after me;
And whirl Fate with me wherefoe'er I fly:
As Winds drive Storms before 'em in the Sky.   [*Exit.*

   Zul. Let not this Infolent unpunifh'd go;
Give your Commands; your Juftice is too flow.
       [Zulema, Hamet *and others are going after him.*
   Abdal. Stay; and what Part he pleafes let him take:
I know my Throne's too ftrong for him to fhake.
But my fair Miftrefs I too long forget;
The Crown I promis'd is not offer'd yet.
Without her Prefence all my Joys are vain,
Empire a Curfe, and Life it felf a Pain.   [*Exeunt.*

ACT IV.

Boabdelin, Abenamar, *Guards.*

   Boab. ADvife, or aid, but do not pity me;
       No Monarch born can fall to that degree.
Pity defcends from Kings to all below;
But can, no more than Fountains, upward flow.
Witnefs, juft Heav'n, my greateft Grief has been
I could not make your *Almahide* a Queen.
   Aben. I have too long th'effects of Fortune known,
Either to truft her Smiles, or fear her Frown.
Since in their firft Attempt you were not flain,
Your Safety bodes you yet a fecond Reign.
The People like a headlong Torrent go,
And ev'ry Dam they break, or overflow;
But unoppos'd they either lofe their Force,
Or wind in Volumes to their former Courfe.
   Boab. In Walls we meanly muft our Hopes inclofe,
To wait our Friends, and weary out our Foes:
While *Almahide*

                                   To

To lawlefs Rebels is expos'd a Prey,
And forc'd the luftful Victor to obey.

Aben. One of my Blood, in Rules of Virtue bred!
Think better of her, and believe fhe's dead.   [*To them Almanzor.*

Boab. We are betray'd, the Enemy is here;
We have no farther room to hope or fear.

Almanz. It is indeed *Almanzor* whom you fee,
But he no longer is your Enemy.
You were ungrateful, but your Foes were more;
What your Injuftice loft you, theirs reftore.
Make Profit of my Vengeance while you may,
My two-edg'd Sword can cut the other way.
I am your Fortune; but am fwift, like her,
And turn my hairy Front if you defer.
That Hour, when you delib'rate, is too late;
I point you the white Moment of your Fate.

Aben. Believe him fent as Prince *Abdalla's* Spy;
He would betray us to the Enemy.

Almanz. Were I, like thee, in Cheats of State grown old,
(Thofe publick Markets, where, for foreign Gold,
The pooreft Prince is to the richeft fold;)
Then thou might'ft think me fit for that low Part:
But I am yet to learn the States-man's Art.
My Kindnefs and my Hate unmask'd I wear;
For Friends to truft, and Enemies to fear.
My Heart's fo p'ain,
That Men on ev'ry paffing through may look,
Like Fifhes gliding in a Chryftal Brook:
When troubled moft, it does the Bottom fhow,
'Tis weedlefs all above, and rocklefs all below.

Aben. E'er he be trufted let him then be try'd;
He may be falfe who once has chang'd his Side.

Almanz. In that you more accufe your felves than me:
None who are injur'd can unconftant be.
You were unconftant; you, who did the Wrong;
To do me Juftice does to me belong.
Great Souls by Kindnefs only can be ty'd;
Injur'd again, again I'll leave your Side.
Honour is what my felf and Friends I owe;
And none can lofe it who forfake a Foe.
Since, then, your Foes now happen to be mine,
Though not in Friendfhip, we'll in Int'reft join.
So, while my lov'd Revenge is full and high,
I'll give you back your Kingdom by the by.
        Boabdelin embracing him.
That I fo long delay'd what you defire,
Was not to doubt your Worth, but to admire,

                                 Almanz.

Almanz. This Counsellor an old Man's Caution shows,
Who fears that little he has left to lose :
Age sets Fortune; while Youth boldly throws.
But let us first your drooping Soldiers chear,
Then seek out Danger, e'er it dare appear.
This Hour I fix your Crown upon your Brow,
Next Hour Fate gives it, but I give it now.   [*Exeunt.*

SCENE II.

Lyndaraxa alone.

O could I read the dark Decrees of Fate,
That I might once know whom to love or hate !
For I my self scarce my own Thoughts can guess,
So much I find them vary'd by Success.
As in some Weather-glass my Love I hold;
Which falls or rises with the Heat or Cold.
I will be constant yet, if Fortune can;
I love the King, let her but name the Man.
                    To her Halyma.

Hal. Madam, a Gentleman, to me unknown,
Desires that he may speak with you alone.

Lyndar. Some Message from the King: Let him appear.
                    To her Abdelmelech; *who, Entring, throws off his Disguise.*
                              She starts.

Abdelm. I see you are amaz'd that I am here:
But let at once your Fear and Wonder end;
In the Usurper's Guards I found a Friend,
Who led me to you safe in this Disguise.

Lyndar. Your Danger brings this Trouble in my Eyes.
But what Affair this vent'rous Visit drew ?

Abdelm. The greatest in the World; the seeing you.

Lyndar. The Courage of your Love I so admire,
That, to preserve you, you shall straight retire.
                              [*She leads him to the Door.*
Go, Dear; each Minute does new Dangers bring;
You will be taken; I expect the King.

Abdelm. The King ! the poor Usurper of an Hour,
His Empire's but a Dream of Kingly Pow'r.
I warn you, as a Lover and a Friend,
To leave him e'er his short Dominion end.
The Soldier I suborn'd will wait at Night;
And shall alone be conscious of your Flight.

Lyndar. I thank you, that you so much Care bestow;
But, if his Reign be short, I need not go.

G   For

For why fhould I expofe my Life and yours,
For what, you fay, a little Time affures?

    Abdelm. My Danger in th' Attemt is very fmall:
And, if he loves you, yours is none at all.
But, though his Ruin be as fure as Fate,
Your proof of Love to me would come too late.
This Trial I, in Kindnefs, would allow;
'Tis eafie, if you love me, fhow it now.

    Lyndar. It is becaufe I love you, I refufe;
For all the World my Conduct would accufe,
If I fhould go, with him I love, away:
And therefore, in ftrict Virtue, I will ftay.

    Abdelm. You would in vain diffemble Love to me:
Through that thin Veil your Artifice I fee.
You would expect th' Event, and then declare:
But do not, do not drive me to Defpair.
For, if you now refufe with me to fly,
Rather than love you after this I'll die·
And therefore weigh it well before you fpeak;
My King is fafe, his Force within not weak.

    Lyndar. The Counfel you have giv'n me, may be wife:
But, fince th' Affair is great, I will advife.

    Abdelm. Then that Delay I for Denial take.────   *[Is going.*

    Lyndar. Stay, you too fwift an Expofition make.
If I fhould go, fince *Zulema* will ftay,
I fhould my Brother to the King betray.

    Abdelm. There is no Fear; but, if there were, I fee
You value ftill your Brother more than me.
Farewel; fome Eafe I in your Falfhood find;
It lets a Beam in, that will clear my Mind.
My Former Weaknefs I with Shame confefs,
And when I fee you next fhall love you lefs.   *[Is going again.*

    Lyndar. Your faithlefs Dealings you may blufh to tell: *[Weeping.*
This is a Maid's Reward, who loves too well.   *[He looks back.*
Remember that I drew my lateft Breath
In charging your Unkindnefs with my Death.

      Abdelm. *coming back.*
    Have I not anfwer'd all you can invent,
Ev'n the leaft fhadow of an Argument?

    Lyndar. You want not Cunning what you pleafe to prove;
But my poor Heart knows only how to love.
And, finding this, you Tyrannize the more:
'Tis plain, fome other Miftrefs you adore;
And now, with ftudy'd Tricks of Subtilty,
You come prepar'd to lay the Fault on me.   *[Wringing her Hands.*

                                      But

But oh, that I fhould love fo falfe a Man!

Abdelm. Hear me, and then difprove it, if you can.

Lyndar. I'll hear no more, your Breach of Faith is plain:
You would with Wit your want of Love maintain.
But, by my own Experience, I can tell,
They who love truly cannot argue well.
Go, Faithlefs Man!
Leave me alone to mourn my Mifery.
I cannot ceafe to love you, but I'll die.

[*Leans her Head on his Arm.*

Abdelm. What Man but I fo long unmov'd could hear [*Weeping.*
Such tender Paffion, and refufe a Tear!
But do not talk of dying any moie,
Unlefs you mean that I fhould die before.

Lyndar. I fear your feign'd Repentance comes too late
I die to fee you ftill thus obftinate.
But yet, in Death, my Truth of Love to fhow,
Lead me; if I have Strength enough I'll go.

Abdelm. By Heav'n you fhall not go: I will not be
O'ercome in Love or Generofity
All I defire, to end th'unlucky Strife,
Is but a Vow that you will be my Wife.

Lyndar. To tie me to you by a Vow, is hard;
It fhows my Love you as no Tie regard.
Name any thing but that, and I'll agree.

Abdelm. Swear then, you never will my Rival's be.

Lyndar. Nay, prithee, this is hardei than before;
Name any thing, good Deai, but that thing more.

Abdelm. Now I too late perceive I am undone:
Living and feeing, to my Death I run.
I know you falfe, yet in your Snares I fall;
You grant me nothing, and I grant you all.

Lyndar. I would grant all; but I muft curb my Will,
Becaufe I love to keep you jealous ftill.
In your Sufpicion I your Paffion find:
But I will take a time to cure your Mind.

Halyma. Oh, Madam, the new King is drawing near!

Lyndar. Hafte quickly hence, left he fhould find you here.

Abdelm. How much more wretched than I came, I go:
I more my Weaknefs and your Falfhood know,
And now muft leave you with my greateft Foe!

[*Exit* Abdelmelech.

Lyndar. Go, how I love thee Heav'n can only tell.
And yet I love thee, foi a Subject, well.——
Yet, whatfoever Charms a Crown can bring,
A Subject's greater than a little King.

I

I will attend 'till time this Throne secure;
And, when I climb, my Footing shall be sure.   [*Musick without.*
Musick! and, I believe, address'd to me.

SONG.

1.

WHERE ever I am, and what ever I do,
    My Phillis is still in my Mind ·
When angry I mean not to Phillis to go,
    My Feet of themselves the Way find ·
Unknown to my self I am just at her Door,
And, when I would rail, I can bring out no more,
    Than Phillis, too Fair and Unkind!

2.

When Phillis I see, my Heart bounds in my Breast,
    And the Love I would stifle is shown:
But asleep, or awake, I am never at rest,
    When from my Eyes Phillis is gone:
Sometimes a sad Dream does delude my sad Mind;
But, alas, when I wake, and no Phillis I find,
    How I sigh to my self all alone!

3.

Should a King be my Rival in her I adore,
    He should offer his Treasure in vain.
O let me alone to be happy and poor,
    And give me my Phillis again!
Let Phillis be mine, and but ever be kind,
I could to a Desart with her be confin'd,
    And envy no Monarch his Reign.

4.

Alas, I discover too much of my Love,
    And she too well knows her own Pow'r!
She makes me each Day a new Martyrdom prove,
    And makes me grow Jealous each Hour
But let her each Minute torment my poor Mind,
I had rather love Phillis, both False and Unkind,
    Than ever be freed from her Pow'r.

Abdalla

Abdalla *enters with Guards.*

Abdal. Now, Madam, at your Feet a King you fee;
Or, rather, if you pleafe, a Scepter'd Slave:
'Tis juft you fhould poffefs the Pow'r you gave.
Had Love not made me yours, I yet had been
But the firft Subject to *Boabdelin.*
Thus Heav'n declares the Crown I bring, your Due:
And had forgot my Title, but for you.

Lyndar. Heav'n to your Merits will, I hope, be kind;
But, Sir, it has not yet declar'd its Mind.
'Tis true, it holds the Crown above your Head,
But does not fix it 'till your Brother's dead.

Abdal. All, but th' *Alhambra,* is within my Pow'r.
And that my Forces go to take this Hour.

Lyndar. When, with its Keys, your Brother's Head you bring,
I fhall believe you are indeed a King.

Abdal. But, fince th' Events of all things doubtful are,
And, of Events, moft doubtful thofe of War;
I beg to know before, if Fortune frown,
Muft I then lofe your Favour with my Crown?

Lyndar. You'll foon return a Conqueror again,
And therefore, Sir, your Queftion is in vain.

Abdal. I think to certain Victory I move;
But you may more affure it by your Love.
That Grant will make my Arms invincible.

Lyndar. My Pray'rs and Wifhes your Succefs foretel.
Go then, and fight, and think you fight for me;
I wait but to reward your Victory.

Abdal. But if lofe it, muft I lofe you too?

Lyndar. You are too curious, if you more would know.
I know not what my future Thoughts will be.
Poor Women's Thoughts are all *Extempore.*
Wife Men, indeed,
Beforehand a long Chain of Thoughts produce,
But ours are only for our prefent ufe.

Abdal. Thofe Thoughts you will not know, too well declare,
You mean to wait the final Doom of War.

Lyndar. I find you come to quarrel with me now.
Would you know more of me than I allow?
Whence are you grown that great Divinity,
That with fuch eafe into my Thoughts can pry?
Indulgence does not with fome Tempers fute,
I fee I muft become more abfolute.

Abdal. I muft fubmit,
On what hard Terms fo e'er my Peace be bought.

Lyndar. Submit! you fpeak as you were not in Fault.

F is

'Tis evident the Injury is mine;
For why fhould you my fecret Thoughts divine?

Abdal. Yet if we might be judg'd by Reafon's Laws!

Lyndar. Then you would have your Reafon judge my Caufe?
Either confefs your Fault, or hold your Tongue;
For I am fure I'm never in the wrong.

Abdal. Then I acknowledge it.

Lyndar. —————————— Then I forgive.

Abdal. Under how hard a Law poor Lovers live!
Who, like the vanquifh'd, muft their Right releafe:
And, with the lofs of Reafon, buy their Peace.   [*Afide*
Madam, to fhow that you my Pow'r command,
I put my Life and Safety in your Hand:
Difpofe of the *Albayzyn* as you pleafe:
To your Fair Hands I here refign the Keys.

Lyndar. I take your Gift becaufe your Love it fhows;
And faithful *Selin* for *Alcade* chufe.

Abdal. *Selin,* from her alone your Orders take:
This one Requeft, yet, Madam, let me make,
That, from thofe Turrets, you th' Affault will fee;
And Crown, once more, my Arms with Victory.
                                          [*Leads her out.*

      Selin *remains with* Gazul *and* Reduan *his Servants*

Selin. *Gazul,* go tell my Daughter that I wait:
You, *Reduan,* bring the Pris'ner to his Fate. [*Exeunt* Gazul *and* Reduan.
E'er of my Charge I will Poffeffion take,
A bloody Sacrifice I mean to make:
The Manes of my Son fhall fmile this Day,
While I in Blood my Vows of Vengeance pay.

      Enter at one Door Benzayda *with* Gazul, *at the other*
          Ozmyn *bound with* Reduan.

Selin. I fent, *Benzayda,* to glad your Eyes:
Thefe Rights we owe your Brother's Obfequies.
                                          [*To* Gazul *and* Reduan.
You two the curs'd *Abencerrago* bind,
You need no more t' inftruct you in my Mind.
                          [*They bind him to one Corner of the Stage.*

Benz. In what fad Object am I call'd to fhare,
Tell me, what is it, Sir, you here prepare?

Selin. 'Tis what your dying Brother did bequeath,
A Scene of Vengeance, and a Pomp of Death.

Benz. The horrid Spectacle my Soul does fright;
I want the Heart to fee the difmal Sight.

Selin. You are my Principal invited Gueft
Whofe Eyes I would not only feed but feaft:

                         You

You are to fmile at his laft groaming Breath,
And laugh to fee his Eye-balls roll in Death:
To judge the ling'ring Soul's convulfive Strife;
When thick fhort Breath catches at parting Life.

Benz. And of what Marble do you think me made?

Selin. What, can you be of juft Revenge afraid?

Benz. He kill'd my Brother in his own Defence;
Pity his Youth, and fpare his Innocence.

Selin. Art thou fo foon to pardon Murder won?
Can he be innocent who kill'd my Son?
Abenamar fhall mourn as well as I;
His *Ozmyn* for my *Tarifa* fhall die.
But, fince thou plead'ft fo boldly, I will fee
That Juftice thou would'ft hinder done by thee:
　　　　　　　　　　　　　　　[*Gives her his Sword.*

Here, take the Sword, and do a Sifter's part,
Pierce his, fond Girl, or I will pierce thy Heart.

Ozm. To his Commands I join my own Requeft,
All Wounds from you are welcome to my Breaft:
Think only, when your Hand this Act has done,
It has but finifh'd what your Eyes begun.
I thought, with Silence, to have fcorn'd my Doom;
But now your noble Pity has o'ercome·
Which I acknowledge with my lateft Breath;
The firft who e'er began a Love in Death.

　　　Benzayda to Selin.
Alas, what Aid can my weak Hand afford?
You fee I tremble when I touch a Sword:
The Brightnefs dazzles me, and turns my Sight.

Ozm. I'll guide the Hand which muft my Death convey;
My leaping Heart fhall meet it half the way:
Or, if I look, 'tis but to aim lefs right.

　　　Selin to Benzayda.
Wafte not the precious Time in idle Breath.

Benz. Let me refign this Inftrument of Death.
　　　[*Giving the Sword to her Father, and then pulling it back.*
Ah no. I was too hafty to refign:
'Tis in your Hand more mortal than in mine.
　　　　　　　　To them Hamet.

Hamet. The King is from th' *Alhambra* beaten back;
And now preparing for a new Attack:
To favour which, he wills, that, inftantly,
You reinforce him with a new Supply.

　　　Selin to Benzayda.
Think not, although my Duty calls me hence,
That with the Breach of yours I will difpence.

E'er my Return, fee my Commands you do;
Let me find *Ozmyn* dead, and kill'd by you.
Gazul and *Reduan*, attend her ftill;
And, if fhe dares to fail, perform my Will.

[*Exeunt* Selin *and* Hamet.

[Benzayda *looks languifhing on him, with her Sword down.*
Gazul *and* Reduan *ftanding with drawn Swords by her.*

Ozm. Defer not, fair *Benzayda,* my Death:
Looking on you———
I fhould but live to figh away my Breath.
My Eyes have done the Work they had to do:
I take your Image with me, which they drew,
And, when they clofe, I fhall die full of you.

Benz. When Parents their Commands unjuftly lay,
Children are privileg'd to difobey.
Yet from that Breach of Duty I am clear,
Since I fubmit the Penalty to bear.
To die or kill you is th' Alternative;
Rather than take your Life, I will not live.

Ozm. This fhows th' Excefs of Generofity;
But, Madam, you have no Pretence to die.
I fhould defame th' *Abencerrages* Race.
To let a Lady fuffer in my Place.
But neither could that Life you would beftow
Save mine; nor do you fo much Pity owe
To me, a Stranger, and your Houfe's Foe.

Benz. From whence-foe'er their Hate your Houfes drew,
I blufh to tell you, I have none for you.
'Tis a Confeffion which I fhould not make,
Had I more Time to give, or you to take.
But, fince Death's near, and runs with fo much Force,
We muft meet firft, and intercept his Courfe.

Ozm. Oh, how unkind a Comfort do you give!
Now, I fear Death again, and wifh to live.
Life were worth taking, could I have it now;
But 'tis more Good than Heav'n can e'er allow
To one Man's Portion, to have Life and you.

Benz. Sure, at our Births,
Death with our meeting Planets danc'd above;
Or we were wounded by a mourning Love!   [*Shouts within.*

Redu. The Noife returns, and doubles from behind;
It feems as if two adverfe Armies join'd:
Time preffes us.

Gaz. ————————If longer you delay,
We muft, though loth, your Father's Will obey.

Ozm.

Ozm. Hafte, Madam, to fulfil his hard Commands:
And refcue me from their ignoble Hands.
Let me kifs yours, when you my Wound begin;
Then eafie Death will flide with pleafure in.

Benz. Ah, gentle Soldiers, fome fhort time allow,

[*To* Gaz. *and* Red.

My Father has repented him e'er now;
Or will repent him, when he finds me dead.:
My Clue of Life is twin'd with *Ozmyn*'s Thread.

Redu. 'Tis fiᵗal to refufe her, or obey;
But where is our Excufe? what can we fay?

Benz. Say any thing——————
Say, that to kill the Guiltlefs you were loath.
Or if you did, fay, I would kill you both.

Gaz. To difobey our Orders is to die:
I'll do't, who dare oppofe it?

Redu. ——————————That dare I.

[Reduam *ftands before* Ozmyn, *and fights with* Gazul.
[Benzayda *unbinds* Ozmyn, *and gives him her Sword.*

Benz. Stay not to fee the iffue of the Fight;   [Red. *kills* Gaz.
But hafte to fave your felf by fpeedy Flight.

[Ozmyn *kneeling to kifs her Hand.*

Did all Mankind againft my Life confpire,
Without this Blefling I would not retire.
But, Madam, can I go and leave you here?
Your Father's Anger now for you I fear:
Confider you have done too much to ftay.

Benz. Think not of me, but fly your felf away.

Redu. Hafte quickly hence; the Enemies are nigh:
From ev'ry part I fee the Soldiers fly;
The Foes not only our Affailants beat,
But fiercely fally out on their Retreat;
And, like a Sea broke loofe, come on amain.

        To them Abenamar, *and a Party with their Swords drawn,*
            driving in fome of the Enemies.

Aben. Traytors, you hope to fave your felves in vain,
Your forfeit Lives fhall for your Treafon pay.
And *Ozmyn*'s Blood fhall be reveng'd this day.

        Ozmyn *kneeling to his Father.*

Ozm No, Sir, your *Ozmyn* lives, and lives to own,
A Father's Piety to free his Son.   [Abenamar *embracing him.*

Aben. My *Ozmyn*! O thou blefling of my Age!
And art thou fafe from their deluded Rage!
Whom muft I praife for thy Deliverance?
Was it thy Valour, or the work of Chance?

                    H   *Ozm.*

Ozm. Nor Chance nor Valour could deliver me;
But 'twas a noble Pity set me free.
My Liberty and Life,
And what your Happiness you're pleas'd to call,
We to this charming Beauty owe it all.

   Aben. Instruct me, visible Divinity,   [*To her*
Instruct me by what Name to worship thee,
For to thy Virtue I would Altars raise:
Since thou art much above all human Praise.
But see———

Enter Almanzor, his Sword bloody, leading in Almahide
attended by Esperanza.

My other Blessing, *Almahide* is here:
I'll to the King, and tell him she is near.
You, *Ozmyn,* on your fair Deliv'rer wait: ——
And with your private-Joys the publick celebrate.   [*Exeunt.*

Almanzor, Almahide, Esperanza.

   Almanz. The work is done; now, Madam, you are free:
At least, if I can give you Liberty.
But you have Chains which you your self have chose;
And, O, that I could free you too from those.
But, you are free from Force, and have full pow'r
To go, and kill my Hopes and me, this hour.
I see, then, you will go, but yet my toil
May be rewarded with a looking while.

   Almah. Almanzor can from ev'ry Subject raise
New matter for our Wonder and his Praise.
You bound and freed me, but the diff'rence is,
That show'd your Valour; but your Virtue this.

   Almanz. Madam, you praise a Fun'ral Victory,
At whose sad Pomp the Conqueror must die.

   Almah. Conquest attends *Almanzor* ev'ry where,
I am too small a Foe for him to fear:
But Heroes still must be oppos'd by some,
Or they would want occasion to o'ercome.

   Almanz. Madam, I cannot on bare Praises live
Those who abound in Praises seldom give.

   Almah. While I to all the World your Worth make known,
May Heav'n reward the Pity you have shown.

   Almanz. My Love is languishing and starv'd to death,
And would you give me Charity, in Breath?
Pray'rs are the Alms of Church-men to the poor
They send to Heav'n's, but drive us from their Door.

Almah.

Almah. Ceafe, ceafe a Sute
So vain to you and troublefome to me,
If you will have me think that I am free.
If I am yet a Slave my Bonds I'll bear,
But, what I cannot grant, I will not hear.

Almanz. You wo'not hear! you muft both hear and grant:
For, Madam, there's an Impudence in Want.

Almah. Your way is fomewhat ftrange to ask Relief;
You ask with threatning, like a begging Thief.
Once more, *Almanzor,* tell me, am I free?

Almanz. Madam, you are from all the World——but me.
But as a Pyrate, when he frees the Prize
He took from Friends, fees the rich Merchandize,
And, after he has freed it, juftly buys;
So, when I have reftor'd your Liberty,——
But then, alas, I am too poor to buy!

Almah. Nay, now you ufe me juft as Pyrates do.
You free me; but expect a Ranfom too.

Almanz. You've all the Freedom that a Prince can have ·
But Greatnefs cannot be without a Slave.
A Monarch never can in private move;
But ftill is haunted with officious Love.
So fmall an Inconvenience you may bear,
'Tis all the Fine Fate fets upon the Fair.

Almah. Yet Princes may retire, when e'er they pleafe;
And breathe free Air from out their Palaces:
They go fometimes unknown, to fhun their State,
And then, 'tis Manners not to know or wait.

Almanz. If not a Subject then a Ghoft I'll be,
And from a Ghoft, you know, no Place is free.
Afleep, awake, I'll haunt you ev'ry where;
From my white Shrowd groan Love into your Ear.
When in your Lover's Arms you fleep at Night,
I'll glide in Cold betwixt, and feize my Right.
And is't not better, in your Nuptial Bed,
To have a living Lover than a dead?

Almah. I can no longer bear to be accus'd,
As if what I could grant you I refus'd.
My Father's Choice I never will difpute;
And he has chofen e'er you mov'd your Sute.
You know my Cafe, if equal you can be,
Plead for your felf, and anfwer it for me.

Almanz. Then, Madam, in that Hope you bid me live:
I ask no more than you may juftly give:
But in ftrict Juftice there may Favour be
And may I hope that you have that for me?

Almah.

Almah. Why do you thus my secret Thoughts pursue,
Which known, hurt me, and cannot profit you?
Your Knowledge but new Troubles does prepare,
Like theirs who curious in their Fortunes are.
To say I could with more Content be yours
Tempts you to hope; but not that Hope assures.
For since the King has Right,
And favour'd by my Father in his Sute,
It is a Blossom which can bear no Fruit.
Yet, if you dare attempt so hard a Task,
May you succeed; you have my Leave to ask.

   Almanz. I can with Courage now my Hopes pursue,
Since I no longer have to combate you.
That did the greatest Difficulty bring;
The rest are small, a Father and a King!

   Almah. Great Souls discern not when the Leap's too wide,
Because they only view the farther Side.
Whatever you desire you think is near:
But, with more Reason, the Event I fear.

   Almanz. No; there is a necessity in Fate,
Why still the brave bold Man is Fortunate,
He keeps his Object ever full in sight,
And that Assurance holds him firm and right.
True, 'tis a narow Path that leads to Bliss,
But right before there is no Precipice:
Fear makes Men look aside, and then their Footing miss.

   Almah. I do your Merit all the Right I can;
Admiring Virtue in a private Man:
I only wish the King may grateful be,
And that my Father with my Eyes may see.
Might I not make it as my last Request,
(Since humble Carriage sutes a Suppliant best)
That you would somewhat of your Fierceness hide:
That inborn Fire; I do not call it Pride.

   Almanz. Born as I am, still to Command, not Sue,
Yet you shall see that I can beg for you.
And if your Father will require a Crown,
Let him but name the Kingdom, 'tis his own.
I am, but while I please, a private Man;
I have that Soul which Empires first began:
From the dull Crowd, which every King does lead,
I will pick out whom I will chuse to head:
The best and bravest Souls I can select,
And on their Conquer'd Necks my Throne erect.

                                                [*Exeunt.*
                                              ACT

ACT V.

Addalla *alone, under the Walls of the* Albayzyn.

Abdal. WHile she is mine, I have not yet lost all,
But in her Arms shall have a gentle Fall:
Blest in my Love, although in War o'ercome,
I fly, like *Anthony* from *Actium,*
To meet a better *Cleopatra* here.
You of the Watch; you of the Watch; appear.
Soldier above.
Who calls below? What's your Demand?
Abdal. ————————'Tis I :
Open the Gate with speed; the Foe is nigh.
Sold. What Orders for Admittance do you bring?
Abdal. Slave, my own Orders; look, and know the King.
Sold. I know you, but my Charge is so severe
That none, without Exception, enter here.
Abdal. Traytor, and Rebel, thou shalt shortly see
Thy Orders are not to extend to me.
Lyndaraxa above.
What sawcy Slave so rudely does exclaim,
And brands my Subject with a Rebel's Name?
Abdal. Dear *Lyndaraxa,* haste; the Foes pursue.
Lyndar. My Lord, the Prince *Addalla,* is it you?
I scarcely can believe the Words I hear :
Could you so coursely treat my Officer?
Abdal. He forc'd me; but the Danger nearer draws,
When I am enter'd you shall know the Cause.
Lyndar. Enter'd! Why have you any Business here?
Abdal. I am pursu'd, the Enemy is near.
Lynd. Are you pursu'd, and do you thus delay
To save your self? Make haste, my Lord, away.
Abdal. Give me not cause to think you mock my Grief
What Place have I, but this, for my Relief?
Lyndar. This Favour does your Handmaid much oblige.
But we are not provided for a Siege.
My Subjects few; and their Provision thin;
The Foe is strong without, we weak within.
This to my noble Lord may seem unkind,
But he will weigh it in his Princely Mind.:

And

And pardon her, who does Affurance want
So much, fhe blufhes when fhe cannot grant.

Abdal. Yes, you may blufh; and you have caufe to weep,
Is this the Faith you promis'd me to keep?
Ah yet, if to a Lover you will bring
No Succour, give your Succour to a King.

Lyndar. A King is he whom nothing can withftand,
Who Men and Mony can with eafe command.
A King is he whom Fortune ftill does blefs;
He is a King who does a Crown poffefs.
If you would have me think that you are he,
Produce to view your Marks of Sov'raignty.
But if your felf alone for Proof you bring,
You're but a fingle Perfon, not a King.

Abdal. Ingrateful Maid, did I for this rebel?
I fay no more; but I have Lov'd too well.

Lyndar. Who but your felf did that Rebellion move?
Did I e'er promife to receive your Love?
Is it my Fault you are not fortunate?
I love a King, but a poor Rebel hate.

Abdal. Who follow Fortune ftill are in the right ————
But let me be protected here this Night.

Lyndar. The Place to morrow will be circled round;
And then no way will for your Flight be found.

Abdal. I hear my Enemies juft coming on;   [*Trampling within.*
Protect me but one Hour, 'till they are gone.

Lyndar. They'll know you have been here, it cannot be,
That very Hour you ftay will ruin me
For if the Foe behold our Enterview,
I fhall be thought a Rebel too, like you.
Hafte hence; and, that your Flight may profp'rous prove,
I'll recommend you to the Pow'rs above.   [*Exit* Lynd. *from above.*

Abdal She's gone: Ah, faithlefs and ingrateful Maid!
I hear fome tread; and fear I am betray'd.
I'll to the *Spanifh* King; and try if he,
To count'nance his own Right, will fuccour me:
There is more Faith in Chriftian Dogs, than thee.   [*Exit.*

          Ozmyn, Benzayda, Abenamar.

Benz. ———————————————— I wifh
(To merit all thefe Thanks) I could have faid,
My Pity only did his Virtue aid:
'Twas Pity, but 'twas of a Love-fick Maid.
His manly Suff'ring my Efteem did move;
That bred Compaffion, and Compaffion Love.

Ozm. O Bleffing fold me at too cheap a rate!
My Danger was the Benefit of Fate.   [*To his Father.*
                                                  But

But that you may my fair Deliv'rer know,
She was not only born our House's Foe,
But to my Death by pow'rful Reasons-led,
At least, in Justice, she might wish me dead.

Aben. But why thus long do you her Name conceal?

Ozm. To gain Belief for what I now reveal:
Ev'n thus prepar'd, you scarce can think it true,
The Saver of my Life from *Selin* drew
Her Birth, and was his Sister whom I slew.

Aben. No more, it cannot, was not, must not be:
Upon my Blessing, say not it was she.
The Daughter of the only Man I hate!
Two Contradictions twisted in a Fate!

Ozm The mutual Hate which you and *Selin* bore,
Does but exalt her gen'rous Pity more.
Could she a Brother's Death forgive to me,
And cannot you forget her Family?
Can you so ill requite the Life I owe,
To reckon her, who gave it, still your Foe?
It lends too great a Lustre to her Line,
To let her Virtue ours so much out-shine.

Aben. Thou gav'st her Line th'Advantage which they have,
By meanly taking of the Life they gave.
Grant that it did in her a Pity show,
But would my Son be pity'd by a Foe?
She has the Glory of thy Act defac'd:
Thou kill'dst her Brother; but she triumphs last:
Poorly for us our Enmity would cease;
When we are beaten we receive a Peace.

Benz. If that be all in which you disagree,
I must confess 'twas *Ozmyn* conquer'd me.
Had I beheld him basely beg his Life,
I should not now submit to be his Wife.
But when I saw his Courage Death control,
I paid a secret Homage to his Soul,
And thought my cruel Father much to blame,
Since *Ozmyn's* Virtue his Revenge did shame.

Aben. What Constancy canst thou e'er hope to find
In that unstable, and soon conquer'd Mind?
What Piety can'st thou expect from her,
Who could forgive a Brother's Murderer?
Or, what Obedience hop'st thou to be pay'd,
From one who first her Father disobey'd?

Ozm. Nature that bids us Parents to obey,
Bids Parents their Commands by Reason weigh.

And

And you her Virtue by your Praise did own,
Before you knew by whom the Act was done.

Aben. Your Reasons speak too much of Infolence,
Her Birth's a Crime paft Pardon or Defence.
Know, that as *Selin* was not won by thee,
Neither will I by *Selin's* Daughter be.
Leave her, or ceafe henceforth to be my Son·
This is my Will; and this I will have done.   [*Exit* Abenamar.

Ozm. It is a murd'ring Will!
That whirls along with an impetuous fway;
And, like Chain-fhot, fweeps all things in its Way.
He does my Honour want of Duty call,
To that, and Love, he has no Right at all.

Benz. No, *Ozmyn*, no, it is much lefs Ill
To leave me, than difpute a Father's Will:
If I had any Title to your Love,
Your Father's greater Right does mine remove·
Your Vows and Faith I give you back again;
Since neither can be kept without a Sin.

Ozm. Nothing but Death my Vows can give me back.
They are not yours to give, nor mine to take.

Benz. Nay, think not, though I could your Vows refign,
My Love or Virtue could difpenfe with mine.
I would extinguifh your unlucky Fire,
To make you happy in fome new Defire:
I can preferve enough for me and you:
And love, and be unfortunate for two.

Ozm. In all that's good and great·
You vanquifh me fo faft, that in the End
I fhall have nothing left me to Defend.
From ev'ry Poft you force me to remove;
But let me keep my laft Retrenchment, Love.

Benz. Love then, my *Ozmyn*; I will be content   [*Giving her Hand.*
To make you wretched by your own Confent:
Live poor, defpis'd and banifh'd for my Sake,
And all the Burden of my Sorrows take,
For, as for me, in whatfoe'er Eftate,
While I have you I muft be Fortunate.

Ozm. Thus then, fecur'd of what we hold moft dear,
(Each others Love) we'll go——I know not where.
For where, alas, fhould we our Flight begin?
The Foe's without, our Parents are within.

Benz. I'll fly to you; and you fhall fly to me·
Our Flight but to each others Arms fhall be.

To

To Providence and Chance permit the reft;
Let us but love enough and we are bleft.   [*Exeunt*.

   Enter Boabdelin, Abenamar, Abdelmelech, *Guard*.
    Zulema *and* Hamet *Prifoners*.

 Abdelm. They're *Lyndaraxa*'s Brothers; for her fake
Their Lives and Pardon my Requeft I make.

 Boab. Then, *Zulema* and *Hamet*, live, but know
Your Lives to *Abdelmelech*'s Sute you owe.

 Zul. The Grace receiv'd fo much my Hope exceeds,
That Words come weak and fhort to anfwer Deeds.
You've made a Venture, Sir, and Time muft fhow
If this great Mercy you did well beftow.

 Boab. You, *Abdelmelech*, hafte, before 'tis Night,
And clofe purfue my Brother in his Flight.

    [*Exeunt* Abdelmelech, Zulema, Hamet.
   Enter Almanzor, Almahide, *and* Efperanza.
But fee, with *Almahide*
The brave *Almanzor* comes, whofe conqu'ring Sword
The Crown it once took from me has reftor'd,
How can I recompence fo great Defert!

 Almanz. I bring you, Sir, perform'd in ev'ry Part
My Promife made; your Foes are fled or flain;
Without a Rival, abfolute you reign.
Yet though, in Juftice, this enough may be,
It is too little to be done by me:
I beg to go
Where my own Courage and your Fortune calls,
To chafe thefe Misbelievers from our Walls.
I cannot breathe within this narrow Space;
My Heart's too big, and fwells beyond the Place.

 Boab. You can perform, brave Warrior, what you pleafe;
Fate liftens to your Voice, and then decrees.
Now I no longer fear the *Spanifh* Pow'rs,
Already we are free, and Conquerors.

 Almanz. Accept, great King, to morrow, from my Hand,
The captive Head of conquer'd *Ferdinand*.
You fhall not only what you loft regain,
But, o'er the *Bifcayn* Mountains to the Main,
Extend your Sway, where never *Moor* did reign.

 Aben. What in another Vanity would feem,
Appears but noble Confidence in him.
No haughty Boafting; but a Manly Pride:
A Soul too fiery, and too great to guide:
He moves excentrique, like a wand'ring Star,
Whofe Motion's juft, tho' 'tis not regular.

     I   *Boab.*

Boab. It is for you, brave Man, and only you,
Greatly to speak, and yet more greatly do.
But, if your Benefits too far extend,
I must be left ungrateful in the End.
Yet somewhat I would pay
Before my Debts above all reck'ning grow,
To keep me from the Shame of what I owe.
But you————
Are conscious to your self of such Desert,
That of your Gift I fear to offer part.

   Almanz. When I shall have declar'd my high Request,
So much Presumption there will be confest,
That you will find your Gifts I do not shun;
But rather much o'er-rate the Service done.

   Boab. Give wing to your Desires, and let em fly
Secure, they cannot mount a pitch too high.
So bless me, *Alha,* both in Peace and War,
As I accord, whate'er your Wishes are,
                     [*Almanz. putting one Knee to the Ground.*
Embolden'd by the Promise of a Prince,
I ask this Lady now with Confidence.

   Boab. You ask the only thing I cannot grant.
          [*The King and* Abenamar *look amazedly on each other.*
But, as a Stranger, you are ignorant
Of what by publick Fame my Subjects know;
She is my Mistress:

   Aben. ——————————And my Daughter too.

   Almanz. Believe, old Man, that I her Father knew.
What else should make *Almanzor* kneel to you?
Nor doubt, Sir, but your Right to her was known·
For had you had no Claim but Love alone,
I could produce a better of my own.
            Almahide softly to him.
Almanzor, you forget my last Request:
Your Words have too much Haughtiness express'd.
Is this the humble way you were to move?
            Almanzor to her.
I was too far transported by my Love.
Forgive me, for I had not learn'd to sue
To any thing before, but Heav'n and you.
Sir, at your Feet, I make it my Request———   [*To the King.*
      [*First Line kneeling · Second rising, and boldly.*
Though, without boasting, I deserve her best;
For you her Love with gaudy Title sought,
But I her Heart with Blood and Dangers bought.

                            Boab.

Boab. The Blood which you have shed in her Defence
Shall have, in time, a fitting Recompence:
Or, if you think your Services delay'd,
Name but your Price, and you shall soon be paid.

Almanz. My Price! why, King, you do not think you deal
With one who sets his Services to Sale?
Reserve your Gifts for those who Gifts regard,
And know I think my self above Reward.

Boab. Then sure you are some God-head, and our Care
Must be to come with Incense, and with Pray'r.

Almanz. As little as you think your self oblig'd,
You would be glad to do't, when next Besieg'd.
But I am pleas'd there should be nothing due,
For what I did was for my self, not you.

Boab. You with Contempt on meaner Gifts look down;
And, aiming at my Queen, disdain my Crown.
That Crown restor'd, deserves no Recompence,
Since you would rob the fairest Jewel thence.
Dare not henceforth Ungrateful me to call;
What e'er I ow'd you, this has cancel'd all.

Almanz. I'll call thee thankless King, and perjur'd both:
Thou swor'st by *Alha*; and hast broke thy Oath.
But thou do'st well; thou tak'st the cheapest way;
Not to own Services thou can'st not pay.

Boab. My Patience more than pays thy Service past;
But now this Insolence shall be thy last.
Hence from my Sight, and take it as a Grace
Thou liv'st, and art but banish'd from the Place.

Almanz. Where e'er I go there can no Exile be;
But from *Almanzor's* Sight I banish thee:
I will not now, if thou wou'dst beg me, stay;
But I will take my *Almahide* away.
Stay thou with all thy Subjects here; but know
We leave the City empty when we go.   [*Takes Almahide's Hand.*

Boab. Fall on; take; kill the Traitor.
                    [*The Guards fall on him; he makes at the King*
                    through the midst of them, and falls upon him,
                    they disarm him, and rescue the King.

Almanz. —————————— Base and poor,
Blush that thou art *Almanzor's* Conqueror.
                    [*Almahide wrings her Hands; then turns and veils her Face.*
Farewel, my *Almahide!*
Life of it self will go, now thou art gone,
Like Flies in Winter when they lose the Sun.
                    [*Abenamar whispers the King a little; then speaks aloud.*

I 2   *Aben.*

Aben. Revenge, and taken so secure away,
Are Blessings which Heav'n sends not ev'ry Day.

Boab. I will at leisure now revenge my Wrong;
And, Traitor, thou shalt feel my Vengeance long:
Thou shalt not die just at thy own Desire,
But see my Nuptials, and with Rage expire.

Almanz. Thou dar'st not Marry her while I'm in sight;
With a bent Brow thy Priest and thee I'll fright:
And in that Scene
Which all thy Hopes and Wishes should content,
The Thought of me shall make thee Impotent.

                        [He is led off by Guards.

             Boabdel. *to* Almahide.

As some fair Tulip, by a Storm opprest,
Shrinks up, and folds its silken Arms to Rest;
And, bending to the Blast, all pale and dead,
Hears, from within, the Wind sing round its Head:
So, shrowded up your Beauty disappears,
Unveil, my Love, and lay aside your Fears.
The Storm that caus'd your Fright is past and done.

       *[Almahide *unveiling and looking round for* Almanzor.

So Flow'rs peep out too soon, and miss the Sun.

                       [Turning from him.

Boab. What Myst'ry in this strange Behaviour lyes?

Almah. Let me for ever hide these guilty Eyes,
Which lighted my *Almanzor* to his Tomb;
Or, let 'em blaze to show me there a-Room.

Boab. Heav'n lent their Lustre for a nobler End:
A thousand Torches must their Light attend,
To lead you to a Temple and a Crown.————
Why does my fairest *Almahide* frown?
Am I less pleasing than I was before,
Or is the insolent *Almanzor* more?

Almah. I justly own that I some Pity have,
Not for the Insolent, but for the Brave.

Aben. Though to your King your Duty you neglect,
Know, *Almahide*, I look for more Respect.
And, if a Parent's Charge your Mind can move,
Receive the Blessing of a Monarch's Love.

Almah. Did he my Freedom to his Life prefer,
And shall I Wed *Almanzor*'s Murderer?
No, Sir, I cannot to your Will submit:
Your Way's too rugged for my tender Feet.

Aben. You must be driv'n where you refuse to go.
And taught, by force, your Happiness to know.

                              Almah.

Almah. To force me, Sir, is much unworthy you, [*Smiling scornfully.*
And, when you would, impossible to do.
If Force could bend me, you might think, with Shame,
That I debase the Blood from whence I came.
My Soul is soft, which you may gently lay
In your loose Palm; but when 'tis press'd to stay,
Like Water, it deludes your Grasp, and slips away.

Boab. I find I must revoke what I decreed;
Almanzor's Death my Nuptials must preceed.
Love is a Magick which the Lover ties;
But Charms still end, when the Magician dies.
Go; let me hear my hated Rival's dead;   [*To his Guards.*
And, to convince my Eyes, bring back his Head.

Almah. Go on; I wish no other way to prove
That I am worthy of *Almanzor's* Love.
We will in Death, at least, united be;
I'll shew you I can die as well as he.

Boab. What should I do! when equally I dread
Almanzor living, and *Almanzor* dead!————
Yet, by your Promise, you are mine alone.

Almah. How dare you claim my Faith, and break your own?

Aben. This for your Virtue is a weak Defence:
No second Vows can with your first dispense.
Yet, since the King did to *Almanzor* swear,
And in his Death ingrateful may appear,
He ought, in Justice, first to spare his Life,
And then to claim your Promise as his Wife.

Almah. What e'er my secret Inclinations be,
To this, since Honour ties me, I agree:
Yet I declare, and to the World will own,
That, far from seeking, I would shun the Throne,
And, with *Almanzor,* lead an humble Life;
There is a private Greatness in his Wife.

Boab. That little Love I have, I hardly buy;
You give my Rival all, while you deny.
Yet, *Almahide,* to let you see your Pow'r,
Your lov'd *Almanzor* shall be free this Hour.
You are obey'd, but 'tis so great a Grace,
That I could wish me in my Rival's Place.
                              [*Exeunt King and* Abenamar.

Almah. How bless'd was I before this Fatal Day!
When all I knew of Love, was to obey!
'Twas Life becalm'd, without a gentle Breath,
Though not so cold, yet motionless as Death.
A heavy quiet State; but Love, all Strife,
All rapid, is the Hurricane of Life.

Had

Had Love not fhown me, I had never feen
An Excellence beyond *Boabdelin*.
I had not, aiming higher, loft my Reft;
But with a Vulgar Good been dully bleft:
But, in *Almanzor*, having feen what's rare,
Now I have learnt too fharply to compare;
And, like a Fav'rite, quickly in Difgrace,
Juft knew the Value e'er I loft the Place.

    To her Almanzor *bound and guarded.*

  Almanz. I fee the End for which I'm hither fent, [*Looking down.*
To double, by your Sight, my Punifhment.
There is a Shame in Bonds I cannot bear;
Far more than Death to meet your Eyes I fear.

    Almahide unbinding him.

  That Shame of long continuance fhall not be:
The King, at my Intreaty, fets you free.

  Almanz. The King! my Wonder's greater than before ·
How did he dare my Freedom to reftore?
He like fome Captive Lion ufes me;
He runs away before he fets me free,
And takes a Sanctuary in his Court:
I'll rather lofe my Life than thank him for't.

  Almah. If any Subject for your Thanks there be,
The King expects 'em not; you owe 'em me.
Our Freedoms through each others Hands have paft;
You give me my Revenge in winning laft.

  Almanz. Then Fate commodiously for me has done;
To lofe mine there where I would have it won.

  Almah. *Almanzor*, you too foon will underftand
That what I win is on another's Hand.
The King (who doom'd you to a cruel Fate)
Gave to my Pray'rs both his Revenge and Hate:
But at no other Price would rate your Life,
Than my Confent and Oath to be his Wife.

  Almanz. Would you to fave my Life my Love betray?
Here; take me; bind me; carry me away;
Kill me: I'll kill you if you difobey.   [*To the Guards.*

  Almah. That abfolute Command your Love does give
I take, and charge you by that Pow'r to live.

  Almanz. When Death, the laft of Comforts, you refufe,
Your Pow'r, like Heav'n upon the damn'd, you ufe:
You force me in my Being to remain,
To make me laft, and keep me frefh for Pain.
When all my Joys are gone,
What Caufe can I, for living longer, give,
But a dull, lazy Habitude to live?

         Almah.

Almah. Rafh Men, like you, and impotent of Will,
Give Chance no time to turn, but urge her ftill:
She would repent; you pufh the Quarrel on,
And once becaufe fhe went, fhe muft be gone.

Almanz. She fhall not turn; what is it fhe can do
To recompence me for the Lofs of you?

Almah. Heav'n will reward your Worth fome better way.
At leaft, for me, you have but loft one Day.
Nor is't a real Lofs which you deplore,
You fought a Heart that was engag'd before.
'Twas a fwift Love which took you in his way;
Flew only through your Heart, but made no Stay.
'Twas but a Dream, where Truth had not a Place;
A fcene of Fancy, mov'd fo fwift a Pace,
And fhifted, that you can but think it was:
Let, then, the fhort vexatious Vifion pafs.

Almanz. My Joys, indeed, are Dreams; but not my Pain.
'Twas a fwift Ruin; but the Marks remain.
When fome fierce Fire lays goodly Building wafte,
Would you conclude
There had been none, becaufe the Burning's paft?

Almah. It was your fault that Fire feiz'd all your Breaft;]
You fhould have blown up fome to fave the reft:
But 'tis, at worft, but fo confum'd by Fire
As Cities are, that by their Fall rife higher.
Build Love a Nobler Temple in my place;
You'll find the Fire has but enlarg'd your fpace.

Almanz. Love has undone me, I am grown fo poor,
I fadly view the Ground I had before,
But want a Stock, and ne'er can build it more.

Almah. Then fay what Charity I can allow;
I would contribute, if I knew but how.
Take Friendfhip; or, if that too fmall appear,
Take Love which Sifters may to Brothers bear.

Almanz. A Sifter's Love! that is fo pall'd a Thing,
What Pleafure can it to a Lover bring?
'Tis like thin Food to Men in Feavers fpent;
Juft keeps alive; but gives no Nourifhment.
What Hopes, what Fears, what Tranfports can it move?
'Tis but the Ghoft of a departed Love.

Almah. You, like fome greedy Cormorant, devour
All my whole Life can give you, in an Hour.
What more I can do for you is to die,
And that muft follow, if you this deny.
Since I gave up my Love that you might live,
You, in refufing Life, my Sentence give.

Almanz.

Almanz. Far from my Breaſt be ſuch an impious Thought:
Your Death would loſe the Quiet mine had ſought.
I'll live for you, in ſpight of Miſery:
But you ſhall grant that I had rather die.
I'll be ſo wretched, fill'd with ſuch Deſpair,
That you ſhall ſee, to live was more to dare.

    Almah. Adieu, then, O my Soul's far better Part,
Your Image ſticks ſo cloſe
That the Blood follows from my rending Heart.
A laſt Farewel!
For, ſince a laſt muſt come, the reſt are vain!
Like Gaſps in Death, which but prolong our Pain.
But, ſince the King is now a Part of me,
Ceaſe from henceforth to be his Enemy.
Go now, for Pity go, or, if you ſtay,
I fear I ſhall have ſomething ſtill to ſay.
Thus——I for-ever ſhut you from my Sight.   [*Veils.*

    Almanz. Like one thruſt out in a cold Winter's Night,
Yet ſhivering underneath your Gate I ſtay;
One Look——I cannot go before 'tis Day——
                         [*She beckens him to be gone.*
Not one——Farewel: Whate'er my Suff'rings be
Within, I'll ſpeak Farewel as loud as ſhe;
I will not be out-done in Conſtancy.——
                         [*She turns her Back.*

Then like a dying Conqueror I go;
At leaſt I have look'd laſt upon my Foe.
I go——but, if too heavily I move,
I walk encumber'd with a Weight of Love.
Fain I would leave the Thought of you behind;
But ſtill, the more I caſt you from my Mind,
You daſh, like Water, back, when thrown againſt the Wind.
                                 [*Exit.*

    [*As he goes off the King meets him with* Abenamar,
            they ſtare at each other without ſaluting.
    Boab. With him go all my Fears: A Guard there wait,
And ſee him ſafe without the City Gate.
                 To them Abdelmeſech.
Now, *Abdelmelech,* is my Brother dead?
    Abdelm. Th' Uſurper to the Chriſtian Camp is fled;
Whom as *Granada's* lawful King they own,
And vow, by Force, to ſeat him in the Throne.
Mean time the Rebels in th' *Albayzyn* reſt;
Which is in *Lyndaraxa's* Name poſſeſt.
    Boab. Haſte, and reduce it inſtantly by Force
    Abdelm. Firſt give me leave to prove a milder Courſe:

                                     She

She will, perhaps, on Summons yield the Place.

Boab. We cannot, to your Sute, refufe her Grace.

[*One enters haftily and whifpers* Abenamar.

Aben. How Fortune perfecutes this hoary Head!
My *Ozmyn* is with *Selin*'s Daughter fled.
But he's no more my Son————
My Hate fhall like a *Zegry* him purfue,
'Till I take back what Blood from me he drew.

Boab. Let War and Vengeance be to Morrow's Care:
But let us to the Temple now repair.
A Thoufand Torches make the Mofque more bright:
This muft be mine and *Almahide*'s Night.
Hence, ye importunate Affairs of State,
You fhould not tyrannize on Love, but wait.
Had Life no Love, none would for Bufinefs live;
Yet ftill from Love the largeft Part we give:
And muft be forc'd, in Empire's weary Toil,
To live long Wretched, to be Pleas'd a while.

[*Exeunt.*

K   E P I-

EPILOGUE.

SUccess, which can no more than Beauty last,
Makes our sad Poet mourn your Favours past.
For, since without Desert he got a Name,
He fears to lose it now with greater Shame.
Fame, like a little Mistress of the Town,
Is gain'd with Ease; but then she's lost as soon.
For, as those tawdry Misses, soon or late,
Jilt such as keep 'em at the highest Rate,
(And oft the Lacquey, or the brawny Clown,
Gets what is hid in the loose-body'd Gown;)
So, Fame is false to all that keep her long;
And turns up to the Fop that's brisk and young.
Some wiser Poet now would leave Fame first:
But elder Wits are, like old Lovers, curs'd;
Who, when the Vigour of their Youth is spent,
Still grow more fond, as they grow impotent.
This, some Years hence, our Poet's Case may prove;
But, yet, he hopes, he's young enough to love.
When Forty comes, if e'er he live to see
That wretched, fumbling Age of Poetry,
'Twill be high time to bid his Muse Adieu.
Well he may please himself, but never you.
'Till then, he'll do as well as he began;
And hopes you will not find him less a Man.
Think him not duller for this Year's Delay;
He was prepar'd, the Women were away;
And Men, without their Parts, can hardly play.
If they, through Sickness, seldom did appear,
Pity the Virgins of each Theatre;
For, at both Houses, 'twas a sickly Year!
And pity us, your Servants, to whose Cost,
In one such Sickness, nine whole Months are lost.
Their Stay, he fears, has ruin'd what he writ.
Long Waiting both disables Love and Wit.
They thought they gave him Leisure to do well.
But, when they forc'd him to attend, he fell!
Yet, though he much has fail'd, he begs, to Day,
You will excuse his unperforming Play:
Weakness sometimes great Passion does express;
He had pleas'd better, had he lov'd you less.

Almanzor and *Almahide:*

OR, THE

CONQUEST

OF

GRANADA.

As it is Acted at the

THEATRE-ROYAL.

The Second Part.

Written by *JOHN DRYDEN*, Servant
to His MAJESTY.

——— *Stimulos dedit æmula virtus.*
Lucan.

LONDON,

Printed for *J. Tonson* and *T. Bennet*: And sold by *R. Wel-
lington*, *G. Strahan*, and *B. Lintott*. 1704.

PROLOGUE

To the Second Part of the

Conquest of *Granada*.

THEY who Write Ill, and they who ne'er durst Write,
Turn Criticks, out of meer Revenge and Spight
A Play-House gives 'em Fame; and up there starts,
From a mean Fifth-rate Wit, a Man of Parts
(So Common Faces on the Stage appear
We take 'em in, and they turn Beauties here)
Our Author fears those Criticks as his Fate
And those he Fears, by consequence, must Hate
For they the Traffick of all Wit invade,
As Scriv'ners draw away the Bankers Trade
Howe'er, the Poet's safe enough to Day
They cannot censure an unfinish'd Play
But, as when Vizard-Mask appears in Pit,
Straight ev'ry Man, who thinks himself a Wit,
Perks up, and, managing his Comb with Grace,
With his white Wigg sets off his Nut-brown Face
That done, bears up to th' Prize, and views each Limb,
To know her by her Rigging and her Trim
Then, the whole Noise of Fops to Wagers go,
Pox on her, 't must be she; and, Damm'ee, no
Just so, I Prophesie, these Wits to Day
Will blindly guess at our imperfect Play
With what new Plots our Second Part is fill'd,
Who must be kept alive, and who be kill'd
And as those Vizard-Masks maintain that Fashion,
To sooth and tickle sweet Imagination
So, our dull Poet keeps you on with Masking,
To make you think there's something worth your asking
But when 'tis shown, that which does now delight you,
Will prove a Dowdy with a Face to fright you.

Almanzor

Almanzor and *Almahide:*
OR, THE
CONQUEST
OF
GRANADA
BY THE
SPANIARDS.

The Second PART.

ACT I.

SCENE, *A Camp.*

King Ferdinand, *Queen* Isabella, Alonzo d' Aguilar, *Attendants, Men and Women.*

K. *Ferd.* AT length the Time is come, when *Spain* shall be
From the long Yoke of *Moorish* Tyrants free.
All Causes seem to second our Design,
And Heav'n and Earth in their Destruction join.
When Empire in its Childhood first appears,
A watchful Fate o'er-sees its tender Years,
'Till, grown more strong, it thrusts and stretches out,
And Elbows all the Kingdoms round about:
The Place thus made for its first Breathing free,
It moves again for Ease and Luxury
'Till, swelling by degrees, it has possest
The greater Space, and now crowds up the rest.
When, from behind, there starts some petty State:
And pushes on its now unweildy Fate:
Then, down the Precipice of Time it goes,
And sinks in Minutes, which in Ages rose.

Q. *Isabel.*

Q. Isabel. Should bold *Columbus* in his Search succeed,
And find those Beds in which bright Metals breed;
Tracing the Sun, who seems to steal away,
That, Miser-like, he might alone survey
The Wealth, which he in Western Mines did lay;
Not all that shining Ore could give my Heart
The Joy, this conquer'd Kingdom will impart:
Which, rescu'd from these Misbeliever's Hands,
Shall now, at once, shake off its double Bands
At once to Freedom and true Faith restor'd;
Its old Religion, and its ancient Lord.

K. Ferd. By that Assault which last we made, I find,
Their Courage is with their Success declin'd:
Almanzor's Absence now they dearly buy,
Whose Conduct crown'd their Arms with Victory.

Alonzo. Their King himself did their last Sally guide,
I saw him glist'ring in bright Armour, ride
To break a Lance in Honour of his Bride.
But other Thoughts now fill his anxious Breast,
Care of his Crown his Love has dispossest.

To them Abdalla.

Q. Isabel. But see the Brother of the *Moorish* King;
He seems some News of great Import to bring.

K. Ferd. He brings a specious Title to our side;
Those who would Conquer, must their Foes divide.

Abdal. Since to my Exile you have Pity shown,
And giv'n me Courage, yet to hope a Throne;
While you, without, our Common Foes subdue,
I am not wanting to my self, or you.
But have, within, a Faction still alive;
Strong to assist, and secret to contrive:
And watching each Occasion to foment
The People's Fears into a Discontent:
Which, from *Almanzor's* Loss, before were great,
And now are doubl'd by their late Defeat.
These Letters from their Chiefs, the News assures.

[*Gives Letters to the King.*

K. Ferd. Be mine the Honour; but the Profit yours.

To them the Duke of Arcos, *with* Ozmyn *and* Benzayda
Prisoners.

K. Ferd. That Tertia of *Italians* did you guide,
To take their Post upon the River side?

D. Arcos. All are according to your Orders plac'd:
My chearful Soldiers their Intrenchments haste;
The *Murcian* Foot have ta'en the upper Ground,
And now the City is beleaguer'd round.

K. Ferd

K. *Ferd.* Why is not then their Leader here again?

D. *Arcos.* The Master of *Alcantara* is slain:
But he who slew him here before you stands;
It is that *Moor* whom you behold in Bands.

K. *Ferd.* A braver Man I had not in my Host:
His Murd'rer shall not long his Conquest boast.
But, Duke of *Arcos*, say, how was he slain?

D. *Arcos.* Our Soldiers march'd together on the Plain;
We two rode on, and left them far behind,
'Till, coming where we found the Valley wind,
We saw these *Moors*; who, swiftly as they could,
Ran on, to gain the Covert of a Wood.
This we observ'd; and, having cross'd their Way,
The Lady, out of Breath, was forc'd to stay:
The Man then stood, and straight his Fauchion drew;
Then told us, we in vain did those pursue,
Whom their ill Fortune to Despair did drive,
And yet, whom we should never take alive.
Neglecting this, the Master straight spurr'd on;
But th' active *Moor* his Horse's shock did shun,
And, e'er his Rider from his Reach could go,
Finish'd the Combat with one deadly Blow.
I, to revenge my Friend, prepar'd to fight;
But now our foremost Men were come in sight:
Who soon would have dispatch'd him on the Place,
Had I not sav'd him from a Death so base,
And brought him to attend your Royal Doom.

K. *Ferd.* A Manly Face, and in his Age's Bloom.
But, to content the Soldiers, he must die;
Go, see him executed instantly.

Q. *Isabel* Stay; I would learn his Name before he go;
You, Prince *Abdalla*, may the Pris'ner know.

Abdal. *Ozmyn*'s his Name; and he deserves his Fate;
His Father heads that Faction which I hate.
But, much I wonder, that with him I see
The Daughter of his Mortal Enemy.

Benz. 'Tis true, by *Ozmyn*'s Sword my Brother fell;
But 'twas a Death he merited too well.
I know a Sister should excuse his Fault;
But you know too, that *Ozmyn*'s Death he sought.

Abdal. Our Prophet has declar'd, by the Event,
That *Ozmyn* is reserv'd for Punishment,
For, when he thought his Guilt from Danger clear,
He, by new Crimes, is brought to suffer here.

Benz. In Love, or Pity, if a Crime you find;
We two have sinn'd above all Human Kind.

Ozm.

Ozm. Heav'n in my Punishment has done a Grace;
I could not suffer in a better Place:
That I should die by Christians it thought good,
To save your Father's Guilt, who sought my Blood.   [*To her.*

Benz. Fate aims so many Blows to make us fall,
That 'tis in vain to think to ward 'em all:
And where Misfortunes great and many are,
Life grows a Burden, and not worth our Care:

Ozm. I cast it from me, like a Garment torn,
Ragged, and too undecent to be worn.
Besides, there is Contagion in my Fate;   [*To* Benz.
It makes your Life too much unfortunate.
But, since her Faults are not ally'd to mine,
In her Protection let your Favour shine:
To you, great Queen, I make this last Request;
(Since Pity dwells in ev'ry Royal Breast)
Safe, in your Care, her Life and Honour be:
It is a dying Lover's Legacy.

Benz. Cease, *Ozmyn,* cease so vain a Sute to move;
I did not give you on those Terms my Love.
Leave Me the Care of Me; for, when you go,
My Love will soon instruct me what to do.

Q. Isabel. Permit me, Sir, these Lovers Doom to give:
My Sentence is, They shall together live.
The Courts of Kings,
To all Distress'd should Sanctuaries be,
But most to Lovers in Adversity.
Castile and *Arragon,*
Which long against each other War did move,
My plighted Lord and I have join'd by Love:
And, if to add this Conquest Heav'n thinks good,
I would not have it stain'd with Lovers Blood.

K. Ferd Whatever *Isabella* shall command
Shall always be a Law to *Ferdinand.*

Benz. The Frowns of Fate we will no longer fear:
Ill Fate, Great Queen, can never find us here.

Q. Isabel. Your Thanks some other time I will receive:
Henceforward, safe in my Protection live.
Granada is for Noble Loves renown'd;
Her best Defence is in her Lovers found.
Love's an Heroick Passion, which can find
No room in any base, degen'rate Mind:
It kindles all the Soul with Honour's Fire,
To make the Lover worthy his Desire.
Against such Heroes I Success should fear,
Had we not too an Host of Lovers here.

An

An Army of bright Beauties come with me;
Each Lady shall her Servant's Actions see:
The Fair and Brave on each side shall contest;
And they shall overcome, who love the best.   [*Exeunt Omnes.*

SCENE II.

The Alhambra.

Zulema *solus.*

True, they have pardon'd me; but do they know
What Folly 'tis to trust a pardon'd Foe!
A Blush remains in a forgiven Face,
It wears the silent Tokens of Disgrace·
Forgiveness to the injur'd does belong;
But they ne'er pardon who have done the Wrong.
My hopeful Fortune's lost! and, what's above
All I can name or think, my ruin'd Love!
Feign'd Honesty shall work me into Trust,
And seeming Penitence conceal my Lust.
Let Heav'n's great Eye of Providence now take
One Day of Rest, and ever after wake.
        Enter Boabdelin, Abenamar *and Guards.*
Boab. Losses on Losses! as if Heav'n decreed
Almanzor's Valour should alone succeed.
    Aben. Each Sally we have made, since he is gone,
Serves but to pull our speedy Ruin on.
    Boab. Of all Mankind, the heaviest Fate he bears,
Who the last Crown of sinking Empire wears.
No kindly Planet of his Birth took care:
Heav'n's Out-cast, and the Dross of ev'ry Star!
                [*A tumultuous Noise within.*
        Enter Abdelmelech.
What new Misfortune do these Cries presage?
    Abdelm. They are th' Effects of the mad Peoples Rage.
All in Despair, tumultuously they swarm;
The farthest Streets already take th' Alarm;
The needy creep from Cellars, under-ground,
To them new Cries from Tops of Garrets sound:
The Aged from the Chimneys seek the Cold;
And Wives from Windows helpless Infants hold.
    Boab. See what the many-headed Beast demands.
                [*Exit* Abdelmelech.
Curs'd is that King whose Honour's in their Hands.

L   T]

In Senates, either they too slowly grant,
Or saucily refuse to aid my Want.
And, when their Thrift has ruin'd me in War,
They call their Insolence my want of Care

Arb. Curss'd be their Leaders, who that Rage foment,
And veil, with publick Good, their Discontent
They keep the Peoples Purses in their Hands,
And hector Kings to grant their wild Demands.
But, to each Lure a Court throws out, descend,
And prey on those they promis'd to defend.

Zul. Those Kings who to their wild Demands consent,
Teach others the same way to Discontent
Freedom in Subjects is not, nor can be;
But still, to please 'em, we must call 'em free.
Propriety, which they their Idol make,
Or Law, or Law's Interpreters can shake

Aben. The Name of Common-wealth is popular;
But there the People their own Tyrants are.

Boab But Kings who rule with limited Command,
Have Players Scepters put into their Hand.
Pow'r has no Balance, one Side still weighs down,
And either hoists the Common-wealth or Crown.
And those who think to set the Scale more right,
By various Turnings but disturb the Weight.

Aben. While People tug for Freedom, Kings for Pow'r,
Both sink beneath some foreign Conqueror:
Then Subjects find too late they were unjust,
And want that Pow'r of Kings they durst not trust.

To them Abdelmelech.

Abdelm. The Tumult now is high, and dang'rous grown:
The People talk of rend'ring up the Town;
And swear that they will force the King's Consent.

Boab. What Counsel can this rising Storm prevent?

Abdelm. Their Fright to no Persuasions will give ear
There's a deaf Madness in a Peoples Fear.

Enter a Messenger.

Mess. Their Fury now a middle Course does take
To yield the Town, or call *Almanzor* back.

Boab. I'll rather call my Death.————
Go, and bring up my Guards to my Defence.
I'll punish this outragious Insolence.

Aben. Since blind Opinion does their Reason sway,
You must submit to cure 'em their own way.
You to their Fancies Physick must apply:
Give them that Chief on whom they most rely.

Unde

Under *Almanzor* prosp'rously they fought:
Almanzor therefore must with Pray'rs be brought.

Enter a Second Messenger.

Second Mess. Haste all you can their Fury to asswage·
You are not safe from their rebellious Rage.

Enter a Third Messenger.

Third Mess. This Minute, if you grant not their Desire,
They'll seize your Person, and your Palace Fire.

Abdelm. Your Danger, Sir, admits of no Delay.

Boab. In Tumults People reign, and Kings obey
Go and appease 'em with the Vow I make,
That they shall have their lov'd *Almanzor* back.   [*Exit Abdel.*
Almanzor has th' Ascendant o'er my Fate:
I'm forc'd to stoop to one I fear and hate
Disgrac'd, distress'd, in Exile, and alone,
He's greater than a Monarch on his Throne.
Without a Realm a Royalty he gains;
Kings are the Subjects over whom he Reigns.

[*A Shout of Acclamations within.*

Aben. These Shouts proclaim the People satisfy'd.

Boab. We for another Tempest must provide.
To promise his Return, as I was loath,
So I want Pow'r now to perform my Oath.
L'er this, for *Afruk* he is sail'd from *Spain.*

Aben. The adverse Winds his Passage yet detain,
I heard, last Night, his Equipage did stay
At a small Village, short of *Malaga.*

Boab. *Abenamar*, this Ev'ning thither haste,
Desire him to forget his Usage-past:
Use all your Rhetrick, Promise, Flatter, Pray.

To them Almahide *attended.*

Aben. Good Fortune shows you yet a surer way.
Nor Pray'rs nor Promises his Mind will move,
'Tis inaccessible to all, but Love.

Boab. Oh, thou hast rouz'd a Thought within my Breast,
That will for ever rob me of my Rest.
Ah Jealousie, how cruel is thy Sting!
I, in *Almanzor*, a lov'd Rival bring!
And now, I think it is an equal·Strife,
If I my Crown should hazard, or my Wife.
Where, Marriage, is thy Cure, which Husbands boast?
That, in Possession, their Desire is lost·
Or why have I alone that wretched Taste,
Which, gorg'd and glutted, does with Hunger last?
Custom and Duty cannot set me free,
Ev'n Sin it self has not a Charm for me.

L 2   Of

Of marry'd Lovers I am sure the first,
And nothing but a King could so be curst.

   Almah. What Sadness sits upon your Royal Heart?
Have you a Grief, and must not I have part?
All Creatures else a time of Love possess·
Man only clogs with Cares his Happiness:
And, while he should enjoy his part of Bliss,
With Thoughts of what may be, destroys what is.

   Boab. You guess'd aright, I am oppress'd with Grief·
And 'tis from you that I must seek Relief.   [*To the Company.*
Leave us; to Sorrow there's a Rev'rence due·
Sad Kings like Suns Eclips'd, withdraw from view.

    [*The Attendants go off, and Chairs are set for the King and Queen.*

   Almah. So, two kind Turtles, when a Storm is nigh,
Look up, and see it gath'ring in the Sky
Each calls his Mate to shelter in the Groves,
Leaving, in Murmur, their unfinish'd Loves.
Perch'd on some dropping Branch they sit alone,
And Coo, and hearken to each others Moan.

   Boab. Since, *Almahide,* you seem so kind a Wife,
                       [*Taking her by the Hand.*
What would you do to save a Husband's Life?

   Almah. When Fate calls on that hard Necessity,
I'll suffer Death rather than you shall die.

   Boab. Suppose your Country should in Danger be;
What would you undertake to set it free?

   Almah. It were too little to resign my Breath·
My own free Hand should give me nobler Death.

   Boab. That Hand, which would so much for Glory do,
Must yet do more, for it must kill me too.
You must kill me, for that dear Country's sake,
Or what's all one, must call *Almanzor* back.

   Almah. I see to what your Speech you now direct;
Either my Love or Virtue you suspect.
But know, that when my Person I resign'd,
I was too Noble not to give my Mind·
No more the Shadow of *Almanzor* fear,
I have no room, but for your Image, here.

   Boab. This, *Almahide,* would make me cease to mourn,
Were that *Almanzor* never to return
But now my fearful People mutiny,
Their Clamours call *Amanzor* back, not I
Their Safety, through my Ruin, I pursue;
He must return, and must be brought by you.

   Almah. That Hour, when I my Faith to you did plight,
I banish'd him for ever from my Sight.

                                      His

His Banifhment was to my Virtue due;
Not that I fear'd him for my felf, but you.
My Honour had preferv'd me innocent.
But I would, your Sufpicion to prevent.
Which, fince I fee augmented in your Mind,
I yet more reafon for his Exile find.

 Boab. To your Intreaties he will yield alone·
And, on your Doom, depend my Life and Throne.
No longer therefore my Defires withftand,
Or, if Defires prevail not, my Command.

 Almah. In his Return too fadly I forefee
Th' Effects of your returning Jealoufie,
But, your Command I prize above my Life:
'Tis facred to a Subject and a Wife
If I have Pow'r *Almanzor* fhall return.

 Boab. Curfs'd be that Fatal Hour when I was Born !
    [*Letting go her Hand, and ftarting up.*
You love, you love him, and that Love reveal
By your too quick Confent to his Repeal.
My Jealoufie had but too juft a Ground;
And now you ftab into my former Wound.

 Almah. This fudden Change I do not underftand.
Have you fo foon forgot your own Command?

 Boab. Grant that I did th' unjuft Injunction lay,
You fhould have lov'd me more than to obey.
I know you did this Mutiny defign,
But your Love-plot I'll quickly countermine.
Let my Crown go, he never fhall return,
I, like a Phœnix, in my Neft will burn.

 Almah. You pleafe me well, that in one common Fate
You wrap your felf, and me, and all your State:
Let us no more of proud *Almanzor* hear
'Tis better once to die, than ftill to fear.
And better, many times, to die, than be
Oblig'd paft Payment to an Enemy.

 Boab 'Tis better, but you Wives ftill have one way·
When e'er your Husbands are oblig'd, you pay.

 Almah. Thou, Heav'n, who know'ft it, judge my Innocence.
You, Sir, deferve not I fhould make Defence.
Yet, judge my Virtue by that Proof I gave,
When I fubmitted to be made your Slave.

 Boab. If I have been fufpicious or unkind,
Forgive me; many Cares diftract my Mind,
Love, and a Crown !
Two fuch Excufes no one Man e'er had ;
And each of 'em enough to make me mad:

           But

But now my Reason re-assumes its Throne,
And finds no Safety when *Almanzor's* gone.
Send for him then; I'll be oblig'd, and sue,
'Tis a less Evil than to part with you.
I leave you to your Thoughts, but love me still!
Forgive my Passion, and obey my Will　　　　　[*Exit* Boabdelin.

Almahide *sola.*

My jealous Lord will soon to Rage return;
That Fire his Fear rakes up, does inward burn
But Heav'n, which made me great, has chose for me,
I must th' Oblation for my People be.
I'll cherish Honour, then, and Life despise,
What is not Pure is not for Sacrifice.
Yet, for *Almanzor,* I in secret mourn!
Can Virtue, then, admit of his Return?
Yes; for my Love I will, by Virtue, square,
My Heart's not mine, but all my Actions are.
I'll like *Almanzor* act, and dare to be
As haughty, and as wretched too as he.
What will he think is in my Message meant?
I scarcely understand my own Intent·
But, Silk-worm like, so long within have wrought,
That I am lost in my own Web of Thought.　　　　[*Exit* Almahide.

ACT II.

SCENE, *A Wood.*

Ozmyn *and* Benzayda

Ozm. 'TIS true that our Protection here has been
Th' Effect of Honour in the *Spanish* Queen.
But, while I as a Friend continue here,
I to my Country must a Foe appear.
　Berz. Think not, my *Ozmyn,* that we here remain
As Friends, but Pris'ners to the Pow'r of *Spain.*
Fortune dispenses with your Country's Right;
But you desert your Honour in your Flight
　Ozm. I cannot leave you here, and go away,
My Honour's glad of a Pretence to stay.
　[*A Noise within,* Follow, follow, follow———

Enter

Enter Selin, *his Sword drawn, as pursued.*

Selin. I am pursu'd, and now am spent and done,
My Limbs suffice me not with Strength to run.
And, if I could, alas! what can I save!
A Year, the Dregs of Life too, from the Grave. [*Sits down on the Ground.*
Here will I sit, and here attend my Fate;
With the same hoary Majesty and State
As *Rome*'s old Senate for the *Gauls* did wait.

Benz. It is my Father, and he seems distress'd.

Ozm. My Honour bids me succour the oppress'd:
That Life he sought for his I'll freely give;
We'll die together, or together live.

Benz. I'll call more Succour, since the Camp is near;
And fly on all the Wings of Love and Fear. [*Exit* Benz.

Enter Abenamar *and four or five Moors. He looks, and*
finds Selin.

Aben. Ye've liv'd, and now behold your latest Hour.

Selin. I scorn your Malice, and defie your Pow'r.
A speedy Death is all I ask you now;
And that's a Favour you may well allow.

Ozm. shewing himself.] Who gives you Death shall give it first to me;
Fate cannot separate our Destiny. [*Knows his Father.*
My Father here! then Heav'n it self has laid
The Snare, in which my Virtue is betray'd.

Aben. Fortune, I thank thee, thou hast kindly done,
To bring me back that Fugitive, my Son,
In Arms too, fighting for my Enemy!
I'll do a *Roman* Justice; thou shalt die.

Ozm. I beg not you my forfeit Life would save:
Yet add one Minute to that Breath you gave.
I disobey'd you, and deserve my Fate;
But bury in my Grave two Houses Hate.
Let *Selin* live, and see your Justice done
On me, while you revenge him for his Son.
Your mutual Malice in my Death may cease,
And equal Loss perfuade you both to Peace.

Aben. Yes, Justice shall be done on him and thee:
Haste, and dispatch 'em both immediately. [*To a Soldier.*

Ozm. If you have Honour, (since you Nature want)
For your own sake my last Petition grant,
And kill not a disarm'd, defenceless Foe:
Whose Death, your Cruelty or Fear will show.
My Father cannot do an Act so base.
My Father! I mistake I meant, who was!

Aben. Go, then, dispatch him first who was my Son.

Ozm. Swear but to save his Life, I'll yield my own.

Aben.

Aben. Nor Tears, nor Pray'rs, thy Life or his shall buy.

Ozm. Then, Sir, *Benzayda*'s Father shall not die.

                [*Putting himself before* Selin.

And, since he'll want Defence when I am gone,
I will, to save his Life, defend my own

 Aben. This Justice Parricides, like thee, should have.

    [*Aben. and his Party attack them both.* Ozmyn *Parries*
    his Father's Thrusts, and thrusts at the others.

    Enter Benzayda, *with* Abdalla, *the Duke of* Arcos
            and Spaniards.

Benz. O help! my Father and my *Ozmyn* save!

Abdal. Villains, that Death you have deserv'd, is near

         Ozmyn *stops his Hand.*

Stay, Prince, and know I have a Father here.
I were that Parricide of whom he spoke,
Did not my Piety prevent your Stroke.

         Arcos *to* Aben.

Depart then, and thank Heav'n you had a Son.

Aben. I am not with these Shows of Duty won.

        Ozmyn *to his Father.*

Heav'n knows I would that Life you seek, resign,
But, while *Benzayda* lives, it is not mine.
Will you yet pardon my unwilling Crime?

 Aben. By no Intreaties, by no length of Time
Will I be won, but, with my latest Breath,
I'll curse thee here, and haunt thee after Death.

             [*Exit* Abenamar *with his Party.*

        Ozmyn *kneeling to* Selin.

Can you be merciful to that degree
A to forgive my Father's Faults in me?
Can you forgive
The Death of him I slew in my Defence;
And, from the Malice, sep'rate the Offence?
I can no longer be your Enemy
In short, now kill me, Sir, or pardon me.   [*Offers him his Sword.*
In t' is your Silence my hard Fate appears!

 Selin. I'll answer you, when I can speak for Tears.
But, till I can————————
Imagine what must needs be brought to pass,   [*Embraces him*
My Heart's not made of Marble, nor of Brass
Did I for you a cruel Death prepare,
And have you——have you made my Life your Care!
There is a Shame contracted by my Faults,
Which hinders me to speak my secret Thoughts.
And I will tell you (when that Shame's remov'd)
You are not better by my Daughter lov'd.

                              Benzayda

Benzayda be yours——I can no more.

Ozmyn embracing his Knees.

Bless'd be that Breath which does my Life restore.

Benz. I hear my Father now, these Words confess,
That Name, and that indulgent Tenderness.

Selin. Benzayda, I have been too much to blame,
But, let your Goodness expiate for my Shame·
You *Ozmyn's* Virtue did in Chains adore,
And Part of me was just to him before.
My Son!   [*To him*

   Ozm My Father!

   Selin.——————Since by you I live,
I, for your sake, your Family forgive.
Let your hard Father still my Life pursue;
I hate not him, but for his Hate to you.
Ev'n that hard Father yet may one Day be
By Kindness vanquish'd, as you vanquish'd me
Or, if my Death can quench to you his Rage,
Heav'n makes good use of my remaining Age.

   Abdal. I grieve your Joys are mingled with my Cares.
But all take Interest in their own Affairs.
And therefore I must ask how mine proceed.

   Selin. They now are ripe, and but your Presence need:
For *Lyndaraxa,* faithless as the Wind,
Yet to your better Fortunes will be kind:
For, hearing that the Christians own your Cause,
From thence th' Assurance of a Throne she draws.
And, since *Almanzor,* whom she most did fear,
Is gone, she to no Treaty will give ear,
But sent me her Unkindness to excuse.

   Abdal. You much surprize me with your pleasing News.

   Selin. But, Sir, she hourly does th' Assault expect
And must be lost, if you her Aid neglect.
For *Abdelmelech* loudly does declare
He'll use the last Extremities of War,
Since she refuse the Fortress to resign.

   Abdal. The Charge of hast'ning this Relief be mine.

   Selin. This while I undertook, whether beset,
Or else by Chance, *Abenamar* I met;
Who seem'd in haste returning to the Town.

   Abdal. My Love must in my Diligence be shown.
And, as my Pledge of Faith to *Spain,* this Hour
I'll put the Fortress in your Master's Pow'r.   [*To* Arcos.

   Selin. An open Way from hence to it there lies,
And we with ease may send in large Supplies,

M

Free

Free from the Shot and Sallies of the Town.

D *Arcos.* Permit me, Sir, to share in your Renown;
First to my King I will impart the News,
And then draw out what Succours we shall use.

                                   [*Exit Duke of* Arcos.

    Abdel. Grant that she loves me not, at least I see   [*Aside.*
She loves not others, if she loves not me.
'Tis Pleasure, when we reap the Fruit of Pain,
'Tis only Pride to be belov'd again.
How many are not lov'd, who think they are?
Yet all are willing to believe the Fair;
And, though 'tis Beauty's known and obvious Cheat,
Yet Man's Self-love still favours the Deceit.   - [*Exit Abdalla.*

    Seli. Farewel, my Children, equally so dear,
That I my self am to my self less near.
While I repeat the Dangers of the War,
Your mutual Safety be each others Care.
Your Father, *Ozmyn,* 'till the War be done,
As much as Honour will permit, I'll shun.
If by his Sword I perish, let him know
It was because I would not be his Foe.

    Ozm. Goodness and Virtue all your Actions guide,
You only err in chusing of your side.
That Party I with Honour cannot take;
But can much less the Care of you forsake:
I must not draw my Sword against my Prince,
But yet may hold a Shield in your Defence.
Benzayda, free from Danger, here shall stay;
And, for a Father and a Lover pray.

    Benz. No, no, I gave not on those terms my Heart,
That from my *Ozmyn* I should ever part.
That Love I vow'd, when you did Death attend,
'Tis just that nothing but my Death should end.
What Merchant is it who would stay behind,
His whole Stock ventur'd to the Waves and Wind?
I'll pray for both, but both shall be in sight,
And Heav'n shall hear me pray, and see you fight.

    Seli. No longer *Ozmyn,* combat a Design,
Where so much Love and so much Virtue join.

    Ozm. Then conquer, and your Conquest happy be,   [*To her.*
Both to your self, your Father, and to me.
With bended Knees our Freedom we'll demand
Of *Isabel,* and mighty *Ferdinand.*
Then, while the Paths of Honour we pursue,
We'll interest Heav'n for us in right of you.   [*Exeunt.*

                      SCENE,

SCENE, *The* Albayzyn.

[An Alarm within, then Soldiers running over the Stage.

Enter Abdelmelech *Victorious, with Soldiers.*

Abdelm. Tis won, 'tis won; and *Lyndaraxa,* now,
Who scorn'd to Treat, shall to a Conquest bow.
To ev'ry Sword I free Commission give;
Fall on, my Friends, and let no Rebel live.
Spare only *Lyndaraxa;* let her be
In Triumph led, to grace my Victory.
Since by her Falshood she betray'd my Love,
Great as that Falshood my Revenge shall prove.
     Enter Lyndaraxa, *as frighted, attended by Women.*
Go, take th' Enchantress, and bring her to me bound.
  Lyndar. Force needs not where Resistance is not found·
I come, my self, to offer you my Hands,
And, of my own accord, invite your Bands.
I wish to be my *Abdelmelech's* Slave;
I did but wish, and easie Fortune gave.
  Abdelm. O, more than Woman false ! but 'tis in vain.
Can you e'er hope to be believ'd again?
I'll sooner trust th' *Hyæna* than your Smile;
Or, than your Tears, the weeping Crocodile.
In War and Love none should be twice deceiv'd,
The Fault is mine if you are now believ'd.
  Lyndar. Be over wise, then, and too late repent;
Your Crime will carry its own Punishment.
I am well pleas'd not to be justify'd:
I owe no Satisfaction to your Pride.
It will be more Advantage to my Fame,
To have it said I never own'd a Flame.
  Abdelm. 'Tis true, my Pride has satisfy'd it self.
I have at length escap'd the deadly Shelf.
Th' Excuses you prepare will be in vain,
'Till I am Fool enough to love again.
  Lyndar Am I not lov'd?
  Abdelm. ————————I must, with Shame, avow
I lov'd you once, but do not love you now.
  Lyndar. Have I for this betray'd *Abdalla's* Trust?
You are to me, as I to him, unjust.   *[Angerly.*
  Abdelm 'Tis like you have done much for love of me,
Who kept the Fortress for my Enemy

Lyndar.

Lyndar. 'Tis true, I took the Fortrefs from his Hand;
But, fince, have kept it in my own Command.
   Abdelm. That Act your foul Ingratitude did fhow.
   Lyndar. You are th' ungrateful, fince 'twas kept for you.
   Abdelm. 'Twas kept indeed; but not by your Intent,
For all your Kindnefs I may thank th' Event.
Blufh, *Lyndaraxa,* for fo crofs a Cheat;
'Twas kept for me, when you refus'd to Treat!   [*Ironically*
   Lyndar. Blind Man! I knew the Weaknefs of the Place:
It was my Plot to do your Arms this Grace:
Had not my Care of your Renown been great,
I lov'd enough to offer you to Treat.
She who is lov'd muft little Lets create;
But you bold Lovers are to force your Fate.
This Force you us'd my Maiden Blufh will fave;
You feem'd to take what fecretly I gave.
I knew we muft be conquer'd; but I knew
What Confidence I might repofe in you.
I knew you were too grateful to expofe
My Friends and Soldiers to be us'd like Foes.
   Abdelm. Well; though I love you not, their Lives fhall be
Spar'd out of Pity and Humanity.   -   [*To a Soldier.*
Alferez, go, and let the Slaughter ceafe.
   Lyndar. Then muft I to your Pity owe my Peace!
                         [*Exit the* Alferez.
Is that the tend'reft Term you can afford?
Time was, you would have us'd another Word.
   Abdelm. Then, for your Beauty, I your Soldiers fpare
For though I do not love you, you are Fair.
   Lyndar. That little Beauty why did Heav'n impart
To pleafe your Eyes, but not to move your Heart!
I'll fhrowd this Gorgon from all Human View;
And own no Beauty, fince it charms not you!
Reverfe your Orders, and your Sentence give;
My Soldiers fhall not from my Beauty live.
   Abdelm. Then, from your Friendfhip, they their Lives fhall gain;
Though Love be dead, yet Friendfhip does remain.
   Lyndar. That Friendfhip, which from wither'd-Love does fhoot,
Like the faint Herbage of a Rock, wants root;
Love is a tender Amity, refin'd ·
Grafted on Friendfhip it exalts the kind.
But when the Graff no longer does remain,
The dull Stock lives; but never bears again.
   Abdelm. Then, that my Friendfhip may not doubtful prove,
(Fool that I am to tell you fo) I love.

                                         You

You would extort this Knowledge from my Breaſt;
And tortur'd me ſo long that I confeſt.
Now I expect to ſuffer foi my Sin;
My Monarchy muſt end, and yours begin.

    Lyndar. Confeſs not Love, but ſpare your ſelf that Shame:
And call your Paſſion by ſome other Name.
Call this Aſſault, your Malice, or your Hate;
Love owns no Acts ſo diſproportionate.
Love never taught this Inſolence you ſhow,
To treat your Miſtreſs like a conquer'd Foe.   [*Alferez.*
Is this th'Obedience which my Heart ſhould move?
This Uſage looks more like a Rape than Love.

    Abdelm. What Proof of Duty would you I ſhould give?

    Lyndar. 'Tis Grace enough to let my Subjects live.
Let your rude Soldiers keep Poſſeſſion ſtill;
Spoil, riffle, pillage, any thing but kill.
In ſhort, Sir, uſe your Fortune as you pleaſe;
Secure my Caſtle, and my Perſon ſeize.
Let your true Men my Rebels hence remove;
I ſhall dream on; and think 'tis all your Love.

    Abdelm. You know too well my Weakneſs and your Pow'r.
Why did Heav'n make a Fool a Conqueror?
She was my Slave; 'till ſhe by me was ſhown
How weak my Force was, and how ſtrong her own.
Now ſhe has beat my Pow'r from ev'ry Part,
Made her Way open to my naked Heart: [*To a Soldier.*
Go, ſtrictly charge my Soldiers to retreat:
Thoſe Countermand who aie not enter'd yet.
On Peril of your Lives leave all things free.   [*Exit Soldier.*
Now, Madam, love *Abdalla* more than me.
I only ask, in Duty, you would bring
The Keys of our *Albayzyn* to the King:
I'll make your Terms as gentle as you pleaſe.
        [*Trumpets Sound a Charge within, and Soldiers Shout.*
What Shouts; and what new Sounds of War are theſe?

    Lyndar. Fortune, I hope, has favour'd my Intent   [*Aſide.*
Of gaining Time, and welcome Succours ſent.

       Enter Alferez

    Alferez. All's loſt, and you are fatally deceiv'd:
The Foe is enter'd, and the Place reliev'd.
Scarce fiom the Walls had I drawn off my Men,
When, from theii Camp, the Enemy ruſh'd in:
And Prince *Abdalla* enter'd firſt the Gate.

    Abdelm. I am betray'd, and find it now too late.   [*To her.*
When your proud Soul to Flatteries did deſcend;
I might have known it did ſome Ill portend.

                           The

The weary Seaman ſtormy Weather fears,
When Winds ſhift often, and no Cauſe appears.
You by my Bounty live————
Your Brothers, too, were pardon'd for my ſake,
And this Return your Gratitude does make.————

 Lyndar. My Brothers beſt their own Obligement know;
Without your charging me with what they owe.
But, ſince you think th' Obligement is ſo great,
I'll bring a Friend to ſatisfie my Debt.   [*Looking behind.*

 Abdelm. Thou ſhalt not Triumph in thy baſe Deſign,
Though not thy Fort, thy Perſon ſhall be mine.
    [*He goes to take her · She runs, and cries out Help.*
 Enter Abdalla, *Duke of* Arcos, *Spaniards.* Abdelmelech *retreats
  fighting, and is purſu'd by the adverſe Party off the Stage.*
       [*An Alarm within.*
 Enter again Abdalla *and the Duke of* Arcos *with* Lyndaraxa.

 D. Arcos. Bold *Abdelmelech* twice our *Spaniards* fac'd;
Though much out-number'd; and retreated laſt.

 Abdal. Your Beauty, as it moves no common Fire, [*To* Lyndaraxa.
So it no common Courage can inſpire.
As he fought well, ſo had he proſper'd too,
If, Madam, he, like me, had fought for you.

 Lyndar. Fortune, at laſt, has choſen with my Eyes;
And, where I would have giv'n it, plac'd the Prize.
You ſee, Sir, with what Hardſhip I have kept
This precious Gage, which in my Hands you left.
But 'twas the Love of you which made me fight,
And gave me Courage to maintain your Right.
Now, by Experience, you my Faith may find;
And are to thank me that I ſeem'd unkind.
When your malicious Fortune doom'd your Fall
My Care reſtrain'd you, then, from loſing all.
Againſt your Deſtiny I ſhut the Gate,
And gather'd up the Shipwrecks of your Fate.
I, like a Friend, did ev'n your ſelf withſtand,
From throwing all upon a loſing Hand.

 Abdal. My Love makes all your Acts unqueſtion'd go,
And ſets a Sov'reign Stamp on all you do.
Your Love, I will believe with hood-wink'd Eyes;
In Faith, much Merit in much Blindneſs lyes.
But now, to make you Great as you are Fair,
The *Spaniards* an Imperial Crown prepare.

 Lyndar. That Gift's more welcome, which with you I ſhare:
Let us no time in fruitleſs Courtſhip loſe,
But ſally out upon our frighted Foes.

No Ornaments of Pow'r so please my Eyes
As Purple, which the Blood of Princes dies.

          [*Exeunt. He leading her.*

S C E N E, *The* Alhambra.

Boabdelin, Abenamar, Almahide, *Guards,* &c.

The Queen *wearing a Scarf.*

Aben. My little Journey has successful been;
The fierce *Almanzor* will obey the Queen.
I found him, like *Achilles* on the Shore,
Pensive, complaining much, but threatning more.
And, like that injur'd *Greek,* he heard our Woes:
Which, while I told, a gloomy Smile arose
From his bent Brows· And still, the more he heard,
A more severe and sullen Joy appear'd.
But, when he knew we to Despair were driv'n,
Betwixt his Teeth he mutter'd Thanks to Heav'n.
  Boab. How I disdain this Aid! which I must take,
Not for my own, but *Almahide's* sake.
  Aben. But when he heard it was the Queen who sent,
That her Command repeal'd his Banishment,
He took the Summons with a greedy Joy,
And ask'd me how she would his Sword employ?
Then bid me say, her humblest Slave would come,
From her fair Mouth with Joy to take his Doom.
  Boab. Oh that I had not sent you! though it cost
My Crown! though I, and it, and all were lost!
  Aben. While I, to bring this News, came on before,
I met with *Selin*———
  Boab.—————————I can hear no more.
             Enter Hamet.
  Hamet. Almanzor is already at the Gate,
And Throngs of People on his Entrance wait.
  Boab. Thy News does all my Faculties surprize,
He bears two Basilisks in those fierce Eyes·
And that tame Dæmon which should guard my Throne,
Shrinks at a Genius greater than his own.
        [*Exit* Boabdelin, *with* Aben. *and Guards.*
  Enter Almanzor, *seeing* Almahide *approach him he speaks.*
  Almanz. So *Venus* moves, when to the Thunderer,
In Smiles or Tears, she would some Sute prefer.

                            When

When with her Cestos girt————
And drawn by Doves, she cuts the liquid Skies,
And kindles gentle Fires where-e'er she flies:
To ev'ry Eye a Goddess is confest,
By all the Heav'nly Nation she is blest,
And each with secret Joy admits her to his Breast.

To her bowing.

Madam, your new Commands I come to know:
If yet you can have any where I go.
If to the Regions of the Dead they be,
You take the speediest course to send by me.

Almah. Heav'n has not destin'd you so soon to Rest:
Heroes must live to succour the Distrest.

Almanz. To serve such Beauty all Mankind should live,
And, in our Service, our Reward you give·
But stay me not in Torture, to behold
And ne'er enjoy. As from another's Gold
The Miser hastens, in his own Defence,
And shuns the Sight of tempting Excellence;
So, having seen you once so killing Fair,
A second Sight were but to move Despair.
I take my Eyes from what too much would please:
As Men in Feavers famish their Disease.

Almah. No; you may find your Cure an easier way,
If you are pleas'd to seek it, in your Stay.
All Objects lose by too familiar View,
When that great Charm is gone of being New.
By often seeing me, you soon will find
Defects so many, in my Face and Mind,
That to be freed from Love you need not doubt;
And, as you look'd it in, you'll look it out.

Almanz. I, rather, like weak Armies, should retreat,
And so prevent my more entire Defeat.
For your own sake in Quiet let me go:
Press not too far, on a despairing Foe:
I may turn back, and arm'd against you move,
With all the furious Train of hopeless Love.

Almah. Your-Honour cannot to ill Thoughts give way;
And mine can run no Hazard by your Stay.

Almanz. Do you then think, I can with Patience see
That sov'reign Good possess'd, and not by me?
No; I all Day shall languish at the Sight,
And rave on what I do not see, all Night.
My quick Imagination will present
The Scenes and Images of your·Content:

Almah.

Almah. Thefe are the Day-dreams which wild Fancy yields,
Empty as Shadows are, that fly o'er Fields.
O, whither would this boundlefs Fancy move!
'Tis but the raging Calenture of Love.
Like a diftracted Paffenger you ftand,
And fee, in Seas, imaginary Land,
Cool Groves, and flow'ry Meads, and, while you think
To walk, plunge in, and wonder that you fink.

Almanz. Love's Calenture too well I underftand;
But fure your Beauty is no Fairy-Land!
Of your own Form a Judge you cannot be;
For, Glow-worm like, you fhine, and do not fee.

Almah. Can you think this, and would you go away

Almanz. What Recompence attends me if I ftay?

Almah. You know I am from Recompence debarr'd;
But I will grant your Merit a Reward.
Your Flame's too noble to deferve a Cheat;
And I too plain to practife a Deceit.
I no Return of Love can ever make;
But what I ask is for my Husband's fake:
He, I confefs, has been ungrateful too;
But he and I are ruin'd if you go.
Your Virtue to the hardeft Proof I bring:
Unbrib'd, preferve a Miftrefs and a King.

Almanz. I'll ftop at nothing that appears fo brave;
I'll do't: And now I no Reward will have.
You've giv'n my Honour fuch an ample Field,
That I may die, but that fhall never yield.
Spight of my felf I'll Stay, Fight, Love, Defpair;
And I can do all this, becaufe I dare.
Yet I may own one Suit————
That Scarf, which, fince by you it has been born,
Is blefs'd, like Relicks which by Saints were worn.

Almah. Prefents, like this, my Virtue durft not make,
But that 'tis giv'n you for my Husband's fake.   [*Gives the Scarf.*

Almanz. This Scarf to Honourable Rags I'll wear:
As conqu'ring Soldiers tatter'd Enfigns bear.
But O how much my Fortune I defpife,
Which gives me Conqueft, while fhe Love denies!

[*Exeunt.*

N   A C T

ACT III.

SCENE, *The* Alhambra.

Almahide, Efperanza.

Efper. A Ffected Modefty has much of Pride;
That Scarf he begg'd, you could not have deny'd.
Nor does it fhock the Virtue of a Wife,
When giv'n that Man, to whom you owe your Life.
  Almah. Heav'n knows, from all intent of Ill 'twas free;
Yet it may feed my Husband's Jealoufie;
And, for that caufe, I wifh it were not done.
                    To them Boabdelin; *and walks apart.*
See where he comes, all penfive and alone,
A gloomy Fury has o'er-fpread his Face:
'Tis fo! and all my Fears are come to pafs.
  Boab. Marriage, thou Curfe of Love, and Snare of Life; [*Afide.*
That firft debas'd a Miftrefs to a Wife!
Love, like a Scene, at diftance fhould appear;
But Marriage views the grofs-daub'd Landfkip near.
Love's naufeous Cure! thou cloy'ft whom thou fhouldft pleafe;
And, when thou cur'ft, then thou art the Difeafe.
When Hearts are loofe, thy Chain our Bodies ties;
Love couples Friends; but Marriage, Enemies.
If Love, like mine, continues after thee,
'Tis foon made four, and turn'd by Jealoufie.
No fign of Love in jealous Men remains,
But that which fick Men have of Life; their Pains.
                    Almahide *walking to him.*
Has my dear Lord fome new Affliction had?
Have I done any thing that makes him fad?
  Boab. You! Nothing: You! But let me walk alone!
  Almah. I will not leave you 'till the Caufe be known:
My knowledge of the Ill may bring Relief.
  Boab. Thank ye: You never fail to cure my Grief!
Trouble me not; my Grief concerns not you.
  Almah. While I have Life I will your Steps purfue.
  Boab. I'm out of Humour now; you muft not ftay.
  Almah. I fear it is that Scarf I gave away.
  Boab. No; 'tis not that:————But fpeak of it no more:
Go hence; I am not what I was before.

                                        Almah.

Almah. Then I will make you fo; give me your Hand!
Can you this Preffing, and thefe Tears withftand!

                   [*Boab. fighing, and going off from her.*

Oh Heav'n, were fhe but mine, or mine alone!
Ah, why are not the Hearts of Women known!
Falfe Women to new Joys unfeen can move:
There are no Prints left in the Paths of Love.
All Goods befides by Publick Marks are known;
But what we moft defire to keep, has none.

                   [*Almah. approaching him.*

Why will you in your Breaft your Paffion croud,
Like unborn Thunder rolling in a Cloud?
Torment not your poor Heart, but fet it free;
And rather let its Fury break on me.
I am not marry'd to a God, I know
Men muft have Paffions, and can bear from you.
I fear th'unlucky Prefent I have made!

   Boab. O Pow'r of Guilt! how Confcience can upbraid!
It forces her not only to reveal,
But to repeat what fhe would moft conceal!

   Almah. Can fuch a Toy, and giv'n in Publick too———

   Boab Falfe Woman, you contriv'd it fhould be fo.
That publick Gift in private was defign'd.
The Emblem of the Love you meant to bind.
Hence from my Sight, ungrateful as thou art;
And, when I can, I'll banifh thee my Heart.   [*She Weeps.*

        To them Almanzor *wearing the Scarf:*
             He fees her weep.

   Almanz. What precious Drops are thofe
Which, filently, each others Track purfue,
Bright as young Diamonds in their infant Dew?
Your Luftre you fhould free from Tears maintain;
Like *Egypt,* rich without the help of Rain.
Now curs'd be he who gave this Caufe of Grief;
And double curs'd who does not give Relief.

   Almah. Our common Fears, and publick Miferies,
Have drawn thefe Tears from my afflicted Eyes.

   Almanz. Madam, I cannot eafily believe
It is for any publick Caufe you grieve.
On your fair Face the Marks of Sorrow lye;
But I read Fury in your Husband's Eye.
And, in that Paffion, I too plainly find
That you're unhappy, and that he's unkind.

   Almah. Not new-made Mothers greater Love exprefs
Than he; when with firft Looks their Babes they blefs.

                                        Not

Not Heav'n is more to dying Martyrs kind;
Nor Guardian Angels, to their Charge affign'd.

Boab. O Goodnefs counterfeited to the Life!
O the well acted Virtue of a Wife!
Would you with this my juft Sufpicions blind?
You've giv'n me great occafion to be kind!
The Marks, too, of your fpotlefs Love appear,
Witnefs the Badge of my Difhonour there. ☉

                      [Pointing to Almanzor's *Scarf.*

  Almanz. Unworthy Owner of a Gem fo rare!
Heav'ns, why muft he poffefs, and I defpair!
Why is this Mifer doom'd to all this Store;
He, who has all, and yet believes he's poor?

            Almahide *to* Almanzor.
  You're much too bold, to blame a Jealoufie,
So kind in him, and fo defir'd by me.
The Faith of Wives would unrewarded prove,
Without thofe juft Obfervers of our Love.
The greater Care the higher Paffion fhows,
We hold that deareft we moft fear to lofe.
Diftruft in Lovers is too warm a Sun,
But yet 'tis Night in Love when that is gone.
And, in thofe Climes which moft his fcorching know,
He makes the nobleft Fruits and Metals grow

  Almanz. Yes, there are Mines of Treafure in your Breaft,
Seen by that jealous Sun, but not poffeft.
He, like a Devil among the Blefs'd above,
Can take no Pleafure in your Heav'n of Love.
Go, take her; and thy caufelefs Fears remove,
Love her fo well that I with Rage may die:
Dull Husbands have no Right to Jealoufie:
If that's allow'd, it muft in Lovers be.
              [To the King.

  Boab. The Succour which thou bring'ft me makes thee bold:
But know, without thy Aid, my Crown I'll hold.
Or, if I cannot, I will fire the Place:
Of a full City make a naked Space.
Hence, then, and from a Rival fet me free:
I'll do, I'll fuffer any thing, but thee.

  Almanz. I wo'not go; I'll not be forc'd away:
I came not for thy fake; nor do I ftay.
It was the Queen who for my Aid did fend;
And 'tis I only can the Queen defend.
I, for her fake, thy Scepter will maintain;
And thou, by me, in fpight of thee, fhalt reign.

  Boab. Had I but hope I could defend this Place
Three Days, thou fhou'dft not live to my Difgrace
So fmall a time——
                      Might

Might I poffefs my *Almahide* alone,
I would live Ages out e'er they were gone.
I fhould not be of Love or Life bereft;
All fhould be fpent before, and nothing left.

Almahide *to* Boabdelin.

As for your fake I for *Almanzor* fent,
So, when you pleafe, he goes to Banifhment.
You fhall, at laft, my Loyalty approve:
I will refufe no trial of my Love.

Boab. How can I think you love me, while I fee
That Trophy of a Rival's Victory?
I'll tear it from his Side.

Almanz. ————————— I'll hold it faft
As Life, and when Life's gone, I'll hold this laft:
And, if thou tak'ft it after I am Slain,
I'll fend my Ghoft to fetch it back again.

Almah. When I beftow'd that Scarf, I had not thought,
Or not confider'd, it might be a Fault.
But, fince my Lord's difpleas'd that I fhould make
So fmall a Prefent, I command it back.
Without Delay th'unlucky Gift reftore·
Or, from this Minute, never fee me more.

[Almanzor *pulling it off haftily, and prefenting it to her.*
The Shock of fuch a Curfe I dare not ftand:
Thus I obey your abfolute Command. [*She gives it to the King.*
Muft he the Spoils of fcorn'd *Almanzor* wear?
May *Turnus* Fate be thine, who dar'd to bear
The Belt of murder'd *Pallas*, from afar
May'ft thou be known, and be the Mark of War.
Live, juft to fee it from thy Shoulders torn
By common Hands, and by fome Coward worn. [*An Alarm within.*

Enter Abdelmelech, Zulema, Hamet, Abenamar,
their Swords drawn.

Abdelm. Is this a time for Difcord or for Grief?
We perifh, Sir, without your quick Relief.
I have been fool'd, and am unfortunate,
The Foes purfue their Fortune and our Fate.

Zul. The Rebels with the *Spaniards* are agreed.

Boab. Take Breath, my Guards fhall to the Fight fucceed.

Abenamar *to* Almanzor.

Why ftay you, Sir? The conqu'ring Foe is near:
Give us their Courage, and give them our Fear.

Hamet. Take Arms, or we muft perifh in your Sight.

Almanz. I care not, perifh; for I will not fight.
I wo'not lift my Arm in his Defence:
And yet I wo'not ftir one Foot from hence.

I

I to your King's Defence his Town refign;
This only Spot, whereon I ftand, is mine.   [*To the Queen.*
Madam, be fafe, and lay afide your Fear,
You are, as in a Magick Circle, here.

    Boab. To our own Valour our Succefs we'll owe.
Hafte, *Hamet,* with *Abenamar* to go;
You two draw up, with all the fpeed you may,
Our laft Referves, and yet redeem the Day.
        [*Exeunt* Hamet *and* Abenamar *one Way, the King the*
          other, with Abdelmelech, &c. Alarm within.
        Enter Abdelmelech, *his Sword drawn.*

    Abdelm. *Granada* is no more! th'unhappy King
Vent'ring too far, e'er we could Succour bring,
Was, by the Duke of *Arcos,* Pris'ner made;
And, paft Relief, is to the Fort convey'd.

    Almanz. Heav'n, thou art juft! go, now defpife my Aid.

    Almah. Unkind *Almanzor,* how am I betray'd!
Betray'd by him in whom I trufted moft!
But I will ne'er out-live what I have loft.
Is this your Succour, this your boafted Love!
I will accufe you to the Saints above!
Almanzor vow'd he would for Honour fight;
And lets my Husband perifh in my fight.
            [*Exeunt* Almahide *and* Efperanza.

    Almanz. O, I have err'd; but Fury made me blind:
And, in her juft Reproach, my Fault I find!
I promis'd ev'n for him to fight, whom I——
——But fince he's lov'd by her he muft not die.
Thus, happy Fortune comes to me in vain,
When I my felf muft ruin it again.

    To him Abenamar, Hamet, Abdelmelech, Zulema, *Soldiers.*

    Aben. The Foe has enter'd the *Vermilion* Tow'rs;
And nothing but th'*Alhambra* now is ours.

    Almanz. Ev'n that's too much, except we may have more;
You loft it all to that laft Stake before:
Fate, now come back, thou can'ft not farther get;
The Bounds of thy Libration here are fet.
Thou know'ft this Place,————
And, like a Clock wound up, ftrik'ft here for me,
Now, Chance, affert thy own Inconftancy·
And, Fortune, fight, that thou may'ft Fortune be.
They come; here, favour'd by the narrow Place,   [*A Noife within.*
I can, with few, their grofs Battalion face.
By the dead Wall, you *Abdelmelech,* wind;
Then, charge, and their Retreat cut off behind.   [*Exeunt.*
                          [*An Alarm within.*
                            Enter

Enter Almanzor *and his Party, with* Abdalla *Prisoner.*

Almanz. You were my Friend; and to that Name I owe [*To* Abdal.
The just Regard, which you refus'd to show.
Your Liberty I frankly would restore;
But Honour now forbids me to do more.
Yet, Sir, your Freedom in your Choice shall be;
When you command to set your Brother free.

Abdal. Th'Exchange which you propose, with Joy I take;
An Offer easier than my Hopes could make.
Your Benefits revenge my Crimes to you·
For I my Shame in that bright Mirror view.

Almanz. No more; you give me Thanks you do not owe:
I have been faulty, and repent me now.
But, though our Penitence a Virtue be,
Mean Souls alone repent in Misery.
The Brave own Faults when good Success is giv'n;
For then they come on equal Terms to Heav'n.   [*Exeunt.*

SCENE, *The* Albayzyn.

Ozmyn *and* Benzayda.

Benz. I see there's somewhat which you fear to tell;
Speak quickly, *Ozmyn,* is my Father well;——
——Why cross you thus your Arms, and shake your Head?
Kill me at once, and tell me he is dead.

Ozm. I know not more than you, but fear not less;
Twice sinking, twice I drew him from the Press:
But the victorious Foe pursu'd so fast,
That flying Throngs divided us at last.
As Seamen parting in a general Wreck,
When first the loos'ning Planks begin to crack,
Each catches one, and straight are far disjoin'd,
Some born by Tides, and others by the Wind;
So, in this Ruin, from each other rent,
With heav'd up Hands we mutual Farewels sent;
Methought his Eyes, when just I lost his View,
Were looking Blessings to be sent to you.

Benz. Blind Queen of Chance, to Lovers too severe,
Thou rul'st Mankind, but art a Tyrant there!
Thy widest Empire's in a Lover's Breast.
Like open Seas, we seldom are at rest.
Upon thy Coasts our Wealth is daily cast;
And thou, like Pirates, mak'st no Peace to last.

To them Lyndaraxa, *Duke of* Arcos, *and Guards.*

D. Arcos. We are surpriz'd when least we did suspect;
And justly suffer'd by our own Neglect.

Lyndar.

Lyndar. No; none but I have Reafon to complain;
So near a Kingdom, yet 'tis loft again !
O, how unequally in me were join'd
A creeping Fortune, with a foring Mind !
O Lottery of Fate ! where ftill the wife
Draw Blanks of Fortune, and the Fool's the Prize !
Thefe crofs, ill-fhuffled Lots from Heav'n are fent,
Yet dull Religion teaches us Content.
But, when we afk it where that Blefling dwells,
It points to Pedant Colleges, and Cells.
There, fhows it rude, and in a homely Drefs;
And that proud Want miftakes for Happinefs.   [*A Trumpet within.*

Enter *Zulema.*

Brother ! what ftrange Adventure brought you here?
Zul. The News I bring will yet more ftrange appear.
The little Care you of my Life did fhow,
Has of a Brother juftly made a Foe:
And *Abdelmelech,* who that Life did fave,
As juftly has deferv'd that Love he gave.
Lyndar. Your Bus'nefs cools, while tedioufly it ftays
On the low Theme of *Abdelmelech*'s Praife.
Zul. This I prefent from Prince *Abdalla*'s Hands.
                    [*Delivers a Letter, which fhe reads.*
Lyndar. He has propos'd, (to free him from his Bands)
That, with his Brother, an Exchange be made.
D. Arcos. It proves the fame Defign which we had laid.
Before the Caftle let a Bar be fet;
And, when the Captives on each fide are met,
With equal Numbers chofen for their Guard,
Juft at the time the Paffage is unbarr'd,
Let both at once advance, at once be free.
Lyndar. Th'Exchange I will my felf in Perfon fee.
Benz. I fear to afk, yet would from Doubt be freed;
Is *Selin* Captive, Sir, or is he dead?
Zul. I grieve to tell you what you needs muft know,
He is a Pris'ner to his greateft Foe.
Kept, with ftrong Guards, in the *Alhambra* Tow'r;
Without the Reach ev'n of *Almanzor*'s Pow'r.
Ozm. With Grief and Shame I am at once oppreft.
Zul. You will be more when I relate the reft.
To you I from *Abenamar* am fent;   [*To Ozmyn.*
And you alone can *Selin*'s Death prevent.
Give up your felf a Pris'ner in his ftead,
Or, e'er to morrow's dawn, believe him dead.
Benz. E'er that appear I fhall expire with Grief.
Zul. Your Action fwift, your Counfel muft be brief.

                                          Lyndar.

Lyndar. While for *Abdalla's* Freedom we prepare,
You in each others Breaft unload your Care.

[*Exeunt all but* Ozmyn *and* Benzayda.

Benz. My Wifhes Contradictions muft imply;
You muft not go; and yet he muft not die.
Your Reafon may, perhaps, th'Extreams unite;
But there's a Mift of Fate before my Sight.

Ozm. The two Extreams too diftant are to clofe;
And Human Wit can no Mid-way propofe.
My Duty therefore fhows the neareft way,
To free your Father, and my own obey.

Benz. Your Father, whom fince yours, I grieve to b'
Has loft, or quite forgot a Parent's Name.
And, when at once poffefs'd of him and you,
Inftead of freeing one, will murder two.

Ozm. Fear not my Life; but fuffer me to go:
What cannot only Sons with Parents do!
'Tis not my Death my Father doe's purfue;
He only would withdraw my Love from you.

Benz. Now, *Ozmyn,* now your want of Love I fee:
For would you go, and hazard lofing me?

Ozm. I rather would ten thoufand Lives forfake:
Nor can you e'er believe the Doubt you make.——
——This Night I with a chofen Band will go;
And, by furprize, will free him from the Foe.

Benz. What Foe! ah whither would your Virtue fall!
It is your Father whom the Foe you call.
Darknefs and Rage will no Diftinction make;
And yours may perifh for my Father's fake.

Ozm. Thus, when my weaker Virtue goes aftray,
Yours pulls it back; and guides me in the Way:
I'll fend him word, my Being fhall depend
On *Selin's* Life, and with his Death fhall end.

Benz. 'Tis that indeed would glut your Father's Rage:
Revenge on *Ozmyn's* Youth, and *Selin's* Age.

Ozm. Whate'er I plot, like *Sifyphus,* in vain
I heave a Stone that tumbles down again.

Benz. This Glorious Work is then referv'd for me;
He is my Father; and I'll fet him free.
Thefe Chains my Father for my Sake does wear:
I made the Fault; and I the Pains will bear.

Ozm. Yes; you no doubt have merited thofe Pains:
Thofe Hands, thofe tender Limbs were made for Chains!
Did I not love you, yet it were too bafe
To let a Lady fuffer in my Place.

O   Thofe

Thofe proofs of Virtue you before did fhow
I did admire, but I muft Envy now.
Your vaft Ambition leaves no Fame for me,
But grafps at Univerfal Monarchy.

    Benz. Yes, *Ozmyn,* I fhall ftill this Palm purfue;
I will not yield my Glory, ev'n to you.
I'll break thofe Bonds in which my Father's ty'd:
Or, if I cannot break 'em, I'll divide.
What, though my Limbs a Woman's weaknefs fhow;
I have a Soul as *Mafculine* as you.
And, when thefe Limbs want Strength my Chains to wear,
My Mind fhall teach my Body how to bear.   [*Exit* Benzayda.

    Ozm. What I refolve I muft not let her know;
But Honour has decreed fhe muft not go.
What fhe refolves I muft prevent with care;
She fhall not in my Fame or Danger fhare.
I'll give ftrict Order to the Guards which wait;
That, when fhe comes, fhe fhall not pafs the Gate.
Fortune, at laft, has run me out of Breath;
I have no Refuge, but the Arms of Death:
To that dark Sanctuary I will go:
She cannot reach me when I lye fo low.

SCENE, *The* Albayzyn.

Enter, on one Side, Almanzor, Abdalla, Abdelmelech, Zulema, Hamet.
On the other Side, the Duke of Arcos, Boabdelin, Lyndaraxa, *and their
Party. After which the Bars are opened; and at the fame time* Boabdelin *and* Abdalla *pafs by each other, each to his Party: When* Abdalla *is pafs'd on the other Side, the Duke of* Arcos *approaches the Bars,
and calls to* Almanzor.

    D. *Arcos.* The Hatred of the Brave with Battels ends;
And Foes, who fought for Honour, then are Friends.
I love thee, brave *Almanzor,* and am proud
To have one Hour when Love may be allow'd.
This Hand, in fign of that Efteem, I plight:
We fhall have angry Hours enough to fight.   [*Giving his Hand.*

    Almanz. The Man who dares, like you, in Fields appear,
And meet my Sword, fhall be my Miftrefs here.
If I am proud, 'tis only to my Foes;
Rough but to fuch who Virtue would oppofe.
If I fome Fiercenefs from a Father drew,
A Mother's Milk gives me fome Softnefs too.

                                     D. *Arcos.*

D. Arcos. Since firſt you took, and after ſet me free,
(Whether a Senſe of Gratitude it be,
Or ſome more ſecret Motion of my Mind,
For which I want a Name that's more than Kind)
I ſhall be glad, by what e're means I can,
To get the Friendſhip of ſo brave a Man:
And would your unavailing Valour call,
From Aiding thoſe whom Heav'n has doom'd to fall.
We owe you that Reſpect———
Which to the Gods of Foes beſieg'd was ſhown;
To call you out before we take your Town.

    Almanz. Thoſe whom we love, we ſhould eſteem 'em too,
And not debauch that Virtue which we wooe.
Yet, though you give my Honour juſt Offence,
I'll take your Kindneſs in the better Senſe:
And, ſince you for my Safety ſeem to fear,
I, to return your Bride, ſhould wiſh you here.
But, ſince I love you more than you do me,
In all Events preſerve your Honour free:
For that's your own, though not your Deſtiny.

    D. Arcos. Were you Oblig'd in Honour by a Truſt,
I ſhould not think my own Propoſals juſt.
But ſince you fight for an unthankful King,
What loſs of Fame can Change of Parties bring?

    Almanz. It will, and may with Juſtice too be thought,
That ſome Advantage in that Change I ſought.
And, though I twice have chang'd, for Wrongs receiv'd,
That it was done for Profit, none believ'd.
The King's Ingratitude I knew before;
So that can be no Cauſe of changing more.
If now I ſtand, when no Reward can be;
'Twill ſhow the Fault before was not in me.

    D. Arcos. Yet there is a Reward to Valour due,
And ſuch it is, as may be ſought by you.
That beauteous Queen, whom you can never gain,
While you ſecure her Husband's Life and Reign.

    Almanz. Then be it ſo. Let me have no Return
               [*Here* Lyndaraxa *comes near and hears them.*
From him but Hatred, and from her but Scorn.
There is this Comfort in a noble Fate,
That I deſerve to be more fortunate.
You have my laſt Reſolve, and now farewel:
My boding Heart ſome Miſchief does foretel.
But what it is, Heav'n will not let me know;
I'm ſad to Death, that I muſt be your Foe

                                        D. Arcos.

D. Arcos. Heav'n, when we meet, if fatal it muſt be
To one; ſpare him; and caſt the lot on me.   [*They retire.*

   Lyndar. Ah, what a noble Conqueſt were this Heart!
I am reſolv'd I'll try my utmoſt Art:
In gaining him, I gain that Fortune too
Which he has Wedded, and which I but Wooe.
I'll try each ſecret Paſſage to his Mind;
And Love's ſoft Bands about his Heart-ſtrings wind.
Not his vow'd Conſtancy ſhall 'ſcape my Snare;
While he, without, Reſiſtance does prepare
I'll melt into him e'er his Love's aware.
   [*She makes a geſture of Invitation to*
     Almanzor, who returns again.

   Lyndar. You ſee, Sir, to how ſtrange a Remedy
A perſecuted Maid is forc'd to fly.
Who, much Diſtreſs'd, yet ſcarce has Confidence
To make your noble Pity her Defence.

   Almanz. Beauty, like yours, can no Protection need;
Or, if it ſues, is certain to ſucceed.
To whate'er Service you ordain my Hand,
Name your Requeſt, and call it your Command.

   Lyndar. You cannot, Sir, but know, that my ill Fate
Has made me Lov'd with all th'Effects of Hate·
One Lover would, by force, my Perſon gain;
Which one, as guilty, would by force detain.
Raſh *Abdelmelech's* Love I cannot prize;
And fond *Abdalla's* Paſſion I deſpiſe.
As you are Brave, ſo you are Prudent too,
Adviſe a wretched Woman what to do.

   Almanz. Have Courage, Fair one; put your Truſt in me;
You ſhall, at leaſt from thoſe you hate, be free.
Reſign your Caſtle to the King's Command;
And leave your Love Concernments in my Hand.

   Lyndar. The King, like them, is fierce, and faithleſs too;
How can I truſt him, who has injur'd you?
Keep for your ſelf (and you can grant no leſs)
What you alone are worthy to poſſeſs.
Enter, brave Sir, for, when you ſpeak the Word,
Theſe Gates will open of their own Accord.
The Genius of the Place its Lords will meet;
And bend its Tow'ry Forehead to your Feet.
That little Cittadel, which now you ſee,
Shall, then, the Head of Conquer'd Nations be:
And ev'ry Turret, from your Coming, riſe
The Mother of ſome great Metropolis.

                         Almanz.

Almanz. 'Tis pity Words, which none but Gods should hear.
Should lose their Sweetness in a Soldier's Ear:
I am not that *Almanzor* whom you praise:
But your fair Mouth can fair Ideas raise:
I am a Wretch, to whom it is deny'd
T'accept, with Honour, what I wish with Pride.
And, since I fight not for my self, must bring
The Fruits of all my Conquests to the King.
Lyndar. Say rather to the Queen; to whose fair Name
I know you vow the Trophies of your Fame.
I hope she is as Kind as she is Fair:
Kinder then unexperienc'd Virgins are
To their first Loves; (though she has lov'd before,
And that first Innocence is now no more·)
But, in Revenge, she gives you all her Heart;
(For you are much too Brave to take a Part.)
Though, blinded by a Crown, she did not see
Almanzor greater than a King could be;
I hope her Love repairs her ill made Choice:
Almanzor cannot be deluded twice.
Almanz. No; not deluded; for none count their Gains,
Who, like *Almanzor*, frankly give their Pains.
Lyndar *Almanzor*, do not cheat your self, nor me;
Your Love is not refin'd to that degree.
For, since you have Desires, and those not blest,
Your Love's uneasie, and at little rest.
Almanz. 'Tis true; my own Unhappiness I see:
But who, alas, can my Physician be?
Love, like a lazy Ague, I endure,
Which fears the Water, and abhors the Cure.
Lyndar. 'Tis a Consumption, which your Life does waste:
Still flatt'ring you with Hope 'till Help be past.
But, since of Cure from her you now despair,
You, like consumptive Men, should change your Air.
Love somewhere else, 'tis a hard Remedy;
But yet you owe your self so much to try.
Almanz. My Love's now grown so much a Part of me,
That Life would, in the Cure, endanger'd be.
At least it like a Limb cut off, would show;
And better die than like a Cripple go.
Lyndar. You must be brought like mad-Men to their Cure;
And Darkness first, and next new Bonds endure:
Do you dark Absence to your self ordain:
And I, in Charity, will find the Chain.
Almanz. Love is that Madness which all Lovers have;
But yet 'tis sweet and pleasing so to Rave.

'Tis

'Tis an Enchantment, where the Reafon's bound :
But Paradife is in th' enchanted Ground.
A Palace, void of Envy, Cares and Strife;
Where gentle Hours delude fo much of Life.
To take thofe Charms away, and fet me free,
Is but to fend me into Mifery.
And Prudence, of whofe Cure fo much you boaft,
Reftores thofe Pains, which that fweet Folly loft.

    Lyndar. I would not, like Philofophers, remove,
But fhow you a more pleafing Shape of Love.
You a fad, fullen, froward Love did fee;
I'll fhow him kind, and full of Grayety.
In fhort, *Almanzor,* it fhall be my Care
To fhow you Love; for you but faw Defpair.

    Almanz. I, in the fhape of Love, Defpair did fee.
You, in his Shape, would fhow Inconftancy.

    Lyndar. There's no fuch thing as Conftancy you call:
Faith ties not Hearts; 'tis Inclination all.
Some Wit deform'd, or Beauty much decay'd,
Firft, Conftancy in Love, a Virtue made.
From Friendfhip they that Land-mark did remove;
And, falfely, plac'd it on the Bounds of Love.
Let th' Effects of Change be only try'd:
Court me, in jeft; and call me *Almahide.*
But this is only Counfel I impart;
For I, perhaps, fhould not receive your Heart.

    Almanz. Fair though you are ————
As Summer Mornings, and your Eyes more bright
Then Stars that twinkle in a Winter's Night;
Though you have Eloquence to warm, and move
Cold Age, and praying Hermits into Love;
Though *Almahide* with Scorn rewards my Care;
Yet, than to change, 'tis nobler to defpair.
My Love's my Soul, and that from Fate is free ·
'Tis that unchang'd and deathlefs Part of me

    Lyndar. The Fate of Conftancy your Love purfue!
Still to be faithful to what's falfe to you.
                     [*Turns from him, and goes off angrily.*

    Almanz. Ye Gods, why are not Hearts firft pair'd above,
But fome ftill interfere in others Love!
E'er each, for each, by certain Marks are known,
You mould 'em up in hafte, and drop 'em down.
And while we feek what carelefsly you fort,
You fit in State, and make our Pains your Sport.
                       [*Exeunt on both fides.*

A C T

ACT IV.

SCENE I.

Abenamar, *and Servants.*

Aben. HASte, and conduct the Pris'ner to my Sight.
  [*Exit Servant, and immediately enters with* Selin *bound.*
Aben. Did you, according to my Orders, write? [*To* Selin.
And have you summon'd *Ozmyn* to appear?

Selin. I am not yet so much a Slave to Fear:
Nor has your Son deserv'd so ill of me,
That, by his Death or Bonds, I would be free.

Aben. Against thy Life thou dost the Sentence give:
Behold how short a time thou hast to live.

Selin. Make haste; and draw the Curtain while you may,
You but shut out the Twilight of my Day:
Beneath the Burden of my Age I bend:
You kindly ease me, e'er my Journeys end.
  [*To them a Servant, with* Ozmyn; Ozmyn *kneels.*
        Abenamar *to* Selin.
It is enough: My Promise makes you free:
Resign your Bonds; and take your Liberty.

Ozm. Sir, you are just, and welcome are these Bands;
'Tis all th' Inheritance a Son demands.

Selin. Your Goodness, O my *Ozmyn*, is too great·
I am not weary of my Fetters yet:
Already, when you move me to resign,
I feel 'em heavier on your Feet than mine.
        Another Soldier or Servant.

Sold. A Youth attends you in the outer Room,
Who seems in haste, and does from *Ozmyn* come.

Aben. Conduct him in:——

Ozm. Sent from *Benzayda*, I fear, to me.
        [*To them* Benzayda *in the Habit of a Man.*

Benz. My *Ozmyn* here!

Ozm. ————Benzayda! 'tis she!
Go, Youth, I have no Business for thee here:
Go to th'*Albayzyn*, and attend me there.
I'll not be long away: I prithee go;
By all our Love and Friendship——

Benz. ————————Ozmyn, no.
I did not take on me this bold Disguise,
For Ends so low to cheat your Watchmens Eyes.

When

When I attempted this, it was to do
An Action, to be envy'd ev'n by you:
But you, alas, have been too diligent,
And, what I purpos'd, fatally prevent!
Those Chains, which for my Father I would bear,
I take with less Content, to find you here.
Except your Father will that Mercy show,
That I may wear 'em both for him and you.

   Aben. I thank thee, Fortune; thou hast, in one Hour,
Put all I could have ask'd thee in my Pow'r.
My own lost Wealth thou gav'st not only back,
But driv'st upon my Coast my Pyrat's Wrack.

   Selin. With *Ozmyn's* Kindness I was griev'd before;
But yours, *Benzayda,* has undone me more.

                 Abenamar to a Soldier.
Go fetch new Fetters, and the Daughter bind.

   Ozm. Be just, at least, Sir, though you are not kind.
Benzayda is not, as a Pris'ner, brought;
But comes to suffer for another's Fault.

   Aben. Then, *Ozmyn,* mark, that Justice which I do,
I, as severely, will exact from you.
The Father is not wholly dead in me:
Or you may yet revive it, if it be.
Like Tapers new blown out, the Fumes remain
To catch the Light; and bring it back again.
Benzayda gave you Life, and set you free;
For that, I will restore her Liberty.

   Ozm. Sir, on my Knees I thank you.

   Aben. ————————————*Ozmyn,* hold:
One Part of what I purpose is untold:
Consider, then, it on your Part remains,
When I have broke, not to resume your Chains.
Like an Indulgent Father, I have pay'd
All Debts, which you, my Prodigal, have made.
Now you are clear, break off your fond Design;
Renounce *Benzayda,* and be wholly mine.

   Ozm. Are these the Terms? Is this the Liberty?
Ah, Sir, how can you so inhuman be?
My Duty to my Life I will prefer;
But Life and Duty must give place to her.

   Aben. Consider what you say; for, with one Breath,
You disobey my Will, and give her Death.

   Ozm. Ah, cruel Father, what do you propose!
Must I, then, kill *Benzayda,* or must lose?
I can do neither in this wretched State
The least that I can suffer is your Hate;

                           And

And yet, that's worfe than Death: Ev'n while I fue,
And chufe your Hatred, I could die for you.
Break, quickly, Heart; or let my Blood be fpilt
By my own Hand, to fave a Father's Guilt.

Benz. Hear me, my Lord, and take this wretched Life,
To free you from the Fear of *Ozmyn's* Wife.
I beg but what with eafe may granted be;
To fpare your Son, and kill your Enemy.
Or, if my Death's a Grace too great to give,
Let me, my Lord, without my *Ozmyn* live.
Far from your Sight and *Ozmyn's* let me go;
And take from him a Care, from you a Foe.

Ozm. How, my *Benzayda!* can you thus refign
That Love, which you have vow'd fo firmly mine?
Can you leave me for Life and Liberty?

Benz. What I have done will fhow that I dare die,
But I'll twice fuffer Death, and go away,
Rather than make you wretched by my Stay;
By this my Father's Freedom will be won:
And to your Father I reftore a Son

Selin. Ceafe, ceafe, my Children, your unhappy Strife;
Selin will not be ranfom'd by your Life.
Barbarian, thy old Foe defies thy Rage •   [*To* Aben.
Turn from their Youth thy Malice, to my Age.

Benz. Forbear, dear Father, for your *Ozmyn's* fake;
Do not fuch Words to *Ozmyn's* Father fpeak.

Ozm. Alas, 'tis counterfeited Rage; he ftrives
But to divert the Danger from our Lives.
For I can witnefs, Sir, and you might fee,
How in your Perfon he confider'd me.
He ftill declin'd the Combat where you were;
And you well know it was not out of Fear.

Benz. Alas, my Lord, where can your Vengeance fall?
Your Juftice will not let it reach us all.
Selin and *Ozmyn* both would Suff'rers be;
And Punifhment's a Favour done to me.
If we are Foes, fince you have Pow'r to kill,
'Tis gen'rous in you not to have the Will.
But, are we Foes? Look round, my Lord, and fee;
Point out that Face which is your Enemy.
Would you your Hand in *Selin's* Blood embrue?
Kill him unarm'd, who, arm'd, fhunn'd killing you.
Am I your Foe? Since you deteft my Line,
That hated Name of *Zegry* I refign:
For you, *Benzayda* will her felf difclaim;
Call me your Daughter, and forget my Name.

P

Selin.

Selin. This Virtue would ev'n Savages subdue;
And shall it want the Pow'r to vanquish you?

Ozm. It has, it has: I read it in his Eyes
'Tis now not Anger; 'tis but Shame denies.
A Shame of Error, that great Spirits find,
Which keeps down Virtue struggling in the Mind.

Aben. Yes; I am vanquish'd! The fierce Conflict's past:
And Shame it self is now o'ercome at last.
'Twas long before my stubborn Mind was won;
But, melting once, I on the sudden run.
Nor can I hold my headlong Kindness more,
Than I could curb my cruel Rage before.

               [Runs to Benz. *and embraces her.*

Benzayda, 'twas your Virtue vanquish'd me.
That could alone surmount my Cruelty.

               [Runs to Selin, *and unbinds him.*

Forgive me, *Selin,* my Neglect of you:
But Men, just waking, scarce know what they do.

Ozm. O Father!

Benz.————————Father!

Aben.————————————Dare I own that Name!
Speak, speak it often, to remove my Shame.

               [They all embrace him.

O *Selin,* O my Children, let me go!
I have more Kindness than I yet can show.
For my Recov'ry, I must shun your Sight:
Eyes, us'd to Darkness, cannot bear the Light.

               [He runs in, they following him.

SCENE, *The* Albayzyn.

Almanzor, Abdelmelech, *Soldiers.*

Almanz. 'Tis War again; and I am glad 'tis so;
Success shall now by Force and Courage go.
Treaties are but the Combats of the Brain,
Where still the stronger lose, and weaker gain.

Abdelm. On this Assault, brave Sir, which we prepare,
Depends the Sum and Fortune of the War.
Encamp'd without the Fort the *Spaniard* lies;
And may, in spight of us, send in Supplies.
Consider yet, e'er we attack the Place,
What 'tis to storm it in an Army's Face.

Almanz. The Minds of Heroes their own Measures are,
They stand exempted from the Rules of War.

*The Minds of Heroes their own Measures are,
They stand exempted from the Rules of War.*

One

One Loofe, one Sally of the Heroe's Soul,
Does all the Military Art control.
While tim'rous Wit goes round, or foords the Shore;
He fhoots the Gulph, and is already o'er.
And, when th' Enthufiaftick Fit is fpent,
Looks back amaz'd at what he underwent.   [*Exeunt.*

[*An Alarm within.*

Enter Almanzor *and* Abdelmelech *with their Soldiers.*

Abdelm. They fly, they fly, take Breath and Charge again.

Almanz. Make good your Entrance, and bring up more Men,
I fear'd, brave Friend, my Aid had been too late.

Abdelm. You drew us from the Jaws of certain Fate.
At my Approach——————————
The Gate was open, and the Draw-bridge down;
But when they faw I ftood, and came not on,
They charg'd with Fury on my little Band;
Who, much o'er-power'd, could fcarce the Shock withftand.

Almanz. E'er Night we fhall the whole *Albayzyn* gain.
But fee, the *Spaniards* march along the Plain
To its Relief; you, *Abdelmelech,* go
And force the reft, while I repulfe the Foe.   [*Exit* Almanzor.

Enter Abdalla, *and fome few Soldiers, who
feem fearful.*

Abdal. Turn, Cowards, turn; there is no hope in Flight;
You yet may live, if you but dare to Fight.
Come, you brave few, who only fear to fly:
We're not enough to Conquer, but to Die.

Abdelm. No, Prince; that mean Advantage I refufe:
'Tis in your Pow'r a nobler Fate to chufe.
Since we are Rivals, Honour does command
We fhould not die, but by each others Hand.
Retire; and if it prove my Deftiny   [*To his Men.*
To fall, I charge you let the Prince go free.

[*The Soldiers depart on both fides.*

Abdal. O, *Abdelmelech,* that I knew fome way
This Debt of Honour which I owe, to pay.
But Fate has left this only Means for me,
To die, and leave you *Lyndaraxa* free.

Abdelm. He who is vanquifh'd and is flain is bleft:
The wretched Conqueror can ne'er have Reft:
But is referv'd a harder Fate to prove;
(Bound in the Fetters of diffembled Love.)

Abdal. Now thou art bafe; and I deferve her more:
Without Complaint I will to Death adore.
Dar'ft thou fee Faults, and yet doft Love pretend?
I will even *Lyndaraxa's* Crimes defend.

    Abdelm.

Abdelm. Maintain her Caufe, then, better than thy own:
Than thy ill got, and worfe defended Throne.

                          [*They fight,* Abdalla *falls.*

Abdelm. Now ask your Life.
   Abdal. —————— 'Tis gone; that bufie thing,
The Soul, is packing up, and juft on Wing.
Like parting Swallows, when they feek the Spring.
Like them, at its appointed time, it goes,
And flies to Countries more unknown than thofe.

      Enter Lyndaraxa *haftily, fees them, and is going out again.*
            Abdelmelech *ftopping her.*

No, you fhall ftay and fee a Sacrifice,
Not offer'd by my Sword, but by your Eyes.
From thofe he firft ambitious Poifon drew;
And fwell'd to Empire, for the Love of you.
Accurfed Fair!
Thy Comet-blaze portends a Prince's Fate;
And fuff'ring Subjects groan beneath thy weight.
   Abdal. Ceafe, Rival, ceafe!
I would have forc'd you; but it wo'not be:
I beg you now, upbraid her not for me.
You Faireft, to my Memory be kind: [*To* Lyndaraxa.
Lovers, like me, your Sex will feldom find.
When I ufurp'd a Crown for Love of you,
I, then, did more, than dying now I do.
I'm ftill the fame as when my Love begun:
And, could I now this Fate forefee or fhun,
Would yet do all I have already done.   [*Dies.*
      [*She puts her Handkerchief to her Eyes.*
   Abdelm. Weep on, weep on; for it becomes you now:
Thefe Tears you to that Love may well allow.
His unrepenting Soul, if it could move
Upward, in Crimes, flew fpotted with your Love;
And brought Contagion to the Blefs'd above.
   Lyndar. He's gone, and Peace go with a conftant Mind;
His Love deferv'd I fhould have been more kind.
But then your Love, and greater Worth I knew.
I was unjuft to him, but juft to you.
   Abdelm. I was his Enemy, and Rival too;
Yet I fome Tears to his Misfortunes owe:
You owe him more; weep then, and join with me:
So much is due ev'n to Humanity.
   Lyndar. Weep for this Wretch, whofe Memory I hate!
Whofe Folly made us both unfortunate!

                                  Weep

Weep for this Fool, who did my Laughter move!
This whining, tedious, heavy lump of Love!

Abdelm. Had Fortune favour'd him, and frown'd on me,
I then had been that heavy Fool, not he;
Just this had been my Fun'ral Elegy.
Thy Arts and Falshood I before did know;
But this last Baseness was conceal'd 'till now.
And 'twas no more than needful to be known;
I could be cur'd by such an Act alone.
My Love, half blasted, yet in time would shoot;
But this last Tempest rends it to the Root.

Lyndar. These little Piques, which now your Anger move,
Will vanish, and are only Signs of Love.
You've been too fierce, and, at some other time,
I should not, with such ease, forgive your Crime.
But, in a Day of publick Joy, like this,
I pardon, and forget what e'er's amiss.

Abdelm. These Arts have oft prevail'd, but must no more:
The Spell is ended, and the Enchantment o'er.
You have at last destroy'd, with much ado,
That Love, which none could have destroy'd, but you.
My Love was blind to your deluding Art;
But Blind-men feel, when stabb'd so near the Heart.

Lyndar. I must confess there was some Pity due:
But I conceal'd it out of Love to you.

Abdelm. No, *Lyndaraxa,* 'tis at last too late:
Our Loves have mingl'd with too much of Fate.
I would, but cannot now my self deceive!
O that you still could cheat, and I believe!

Lyndar. Do not so light a Quarrel long pursue:
You grieve your Rival was less lov'd than you.
'Tis hard, when Men of Kindness must complain!

Abdelm. I'm now awake, and cannot Dream again.

Lyndar. Yet hear————

Abdelm. ———— No more; nothing my Heart can bend:
That Queen you scorn'd you shall this Night attend:
Your Life the King has pardon'd for my sake,
But, on your Pride, I some Revenge must take.
See now th' Effects of what your Arts design'd:
Thank your inconstant and ambitious Mind.
'Tis just that she, who to no Love is true,
Should be forsaken, and contemn'd, like you.

Lyndar. All Arts of injur'd Women I will try:
First I will be reveng'd; and then I'll die.
But like some falling Tow'r,————

Whose.

Whose seeming Firmness does the Sight beguile;
So hold I up my nodding Head a while,
'Till they come under; and reserve my Fall,
That with my Ruins I may reach 'em all.

Abdelm. Conduct her hence————

[*Exit* Lyndaraxa *guarded.*

Enter a Soldier.

Sold. Almanzor is Victorious without Fight;
The Foes retreated when he came in sight.
Under the Walls, this Night, his Men are drawn;
And mean to seek the *Spaniard* with the Dawn.

Abdelm. The Sun's declin'd:
Command the Watch be set without delay;
And in the Fort let bold *Benducar* stay:
I'll haste to Court, where Solitude I'll fly;   [*Aside.*
And herd, like wounded Deer, in Company.
But oh, how hard is Passion to remove,
When I must shun my self, to 'scape from Love!   [*Exit.*

SCENE, *The* Alhambra, *or a* Gallery.

Zulema, Hamet.

Hamet. I thought your Passion for the Queen was dead:
Or that your Love had, with your Hopes, been fled.

Zul. 'Twas like a Fire within a Furnace pent:
I smother'd it, and kept it long from Vent.
But (fed with Looks, and blown with Sighs so fast)
It broke a Passage through my Lips at last.

Hamet. Where found you Confidence your Suit to move?
Our broken Fortunes are not fit to love.
Well; you declar'd your Love:——What follow'd then?

Zul. She look'd as Judges do on guilty Men:
When big with Fate they triumph in their Dooms,
And smile before the deadly Sentence comes.
Silent I stood, as I were Thunder-struck;
Condemn'd and executed with a Look.

Hamet. You must, with haste, some Remedy prepare:
Now you are in, you must break through the Snare.

Zul. She said she would my Folly yet conceal,
But vow'd my next Attempt she would reveal.

Hamet. 'Tis dark; and, in this lonely Gallery,
(Remote from Noise, and shunning ev'ry Eye)
One Hour each Ev'ning she, in private mourns,
And prays, and to the Circle then returns.
Now, if you dare attempt her passing by.————

Zul. These lighted Tapers show the time is nigh.

Perhaps

Perhaps my Courtſhip will not be in vain:
At leaſt, few Women will of Force complain.

At the other End of the Gallery, Enter Almanzor *and* Eſperanza.

Hamet. Almanzor, and with him————
The fav'rite Slave of the Sultana Queen:
Zul. E'er they approach, let us retire unſeen;
And watch our Time when they return again:
Then Force ſhall give, if Favour does deny;
And that once done we'll to the *Spaniards* fly.   [*Exeunt.*
    Almanz. Now ſtand; th' Apartment of the Queen is near;
And, from this Place, your Voice will reach her Ear.
                                    [Eſperanza *goes out.*

S O N G, in Two Parts.

He. HOW *unhappy a Lover am I,*
      While I ſigh for my Phillis *in vain;*
All my Hopes of Delight
Are another Man's Right,
      Who is happy while I am in Pain!

2.

She. *Since her Honour allows no Relief,*
      But to pity the Pains which you bear,
'Tis the beſt of your Fate
(In a hopeleſs Eſtate)
      To give o'er, and betimes to deſpair.

3.

He. *I have try'd the falſe Med'cine in vain;*
      For I wiſh what I hope not to win:
From without, my Deſire
Has no Food to its Fire;
      But it burns and conſumes me within.

4.

She. *Yet, at leaſt, 'tis a Pleaſure to know*
      That you are not unhappy alone:
For the Nymph you adore
Is as wretched, and more;
      And counts all your Suff'rings her own.

5.

He. *O ye Gods, let me ſuffer for both;*
      At the Feet of my Phillis *I'll lie*
I'll reſign up my Breath,
And take Pleaſure in Death,
      To be pity'd by her when I die.

                                    6. She.

6.

She. *What her Honour deny'd you in Life,*
In her Death she will give to your Love.
Such a Flame as is true
After Fate will renew,
For the Souls to meet closer above.

Enter Esperanza again after the Song.

Almanz. Accept this Diamond, 'till I can present
Something more worthy my Acknowledgment.
And now farewel   I will attend, alone,
Her coming forth; and make my Suff'rings known   [*Exit Esperanza.*
   Solus.
A hollow Wind comes whistling through that Door,
And a cold Shiv'ring seizes me all o'er:
My Teeth, too, chatter with a sudden Fright:
These are the Raptures of too fierce Delight!
The Combat of the Tyrants, Hope and Fear;
Whtch Hearts, for want of Field-room, cannot bear.
I grow impatient; this, or that's the Room:
I'll meet her; now, methinks, I hear her come.
                              [*He goes to the Door, the Ghost of his*
                                 Mother meets him: He starts back.
                                 The Ghost stands in the Door.
Almanz. Well may'st thou make thy Boast, what e'er thou art,
Thou art the first e'er made *Almanzor* start.
My Legs————
Shall bear me to thee in their own Despight:
I'll rush into the Covert of thy Night,
And pull thee backward by the Shrowd, to Light.
Or else I'll squeeze thee, like a Bladder, there;
And make thee groan thy self away to Air.   [*The Ghost retires.*
So, art thou gone! Thou canst no Conquest boast:
I thought what was the Courage of a Ghost.————
————The grudging of my Ague yet remains:
My Blood, like Isicles, hangs in my Veins,
And does not drop: Be Master of that Door,
We two will not disturb each other more.
I err'd a little, but Extreams may join;
That Door was Hell's, but this is Heav'n's and mine.
          [*Goes to the other Door, and is met again by the Ghost.*
Again! By Heav'n I do conjure thee, speak.
What art thou, Spirit? and what dost thou seek?
          [*The Ghost comes on softly after the Conjuration; and*
              Almanzor retires to the middle of the Stage.

                                                  Ghost.

The ghost of Almanzor's mother (handwritten annotation)

Ghoſt. I am the Ghoſt of her who gave thee Birth?
The airy Shadow of her mould'ring Earth.
Love of thy Father me through Seas did guide,
On Seas I bore thee, and on Seas I dy'd.
I dy'd; and for my winding Sheet a Wave
I had; and all the Ocean for my Grave.
But, when my Soul to Bliſs did upward move,
I wander'd round the Cryſtal Walls above;
But found th' Eternal Fence ſo ſteeply high,
That, when I mounted to the middle Sky,
I flagg'd, and flutter'd down, and could not fly.
Then, form the Battlements of th' Heav'nly Tow'r,
A Watchman Angel bid me wait this Hour,
And told me I had yet a Task aſſign'd,
To warn that little Pledge I left behind;
And to divert him, e'er it were too late,
From Crimes unknown, and Errors of his Fate.
                  Almanzor *bowing.*
  Speak, Holy Shade; thou Parent-form, ſpeak on:
Inſtruct thy Mortal Elemented Son;
(For here I wander, to my ſelf unknown.)
But O, thou better Part of Heav'nly Air,
Teach me, kind Spirit, (ſince I'm ſtill thy Care)
My Parents Names;
If I have yet a Father, let me know,
To whoſe old Age my humble Youth muſt bow;
And pay its Duty, if he Mortal be;
Or Adoration, if a Mind, like thee.
  Ghoſt. Then, what I may, I'll tell————
From ancient Blood thy Father's Lineage ſprings,
Thy Mother's thou deriv'ſt from Stems of Kings.
A Chriſtian born, and born again that Day,
When ſacred Water waſh'd thy Sins away.
Yet, bred in Errors, thou doſt miſ-imploy
That Strength Heav'n gave thee, and its Flock deſtroy.
  Almanz. By Reaſon, Man a God-head may diſcern:
But, how he ſhould be worſhip'd, cannot learn.
  Ghoſt. Heav'n does not now thy Ignorance reprove,
But warns thee from known Crimes of lawleſs Love.
That Crime thou know'ſt, and, knowing, does not ſhun,
Shall an unknown and greater Crime pull on:
But if, thus warn'd, thou leav'ſt this curſed Place,
Then ſhalt thou know the Author of thy Race.
Once more I'll ſee thee. Then my Charge is done.
Far hence, upon the Mountains of the Moon,

Almanzor is noble. (handwritten annotation)

Is my Abode; where Heav'n and Nature smile,
And strew with Flow'rs the secret Bed of *Nile.*
Bless'd Souls are there refin'd, and made more bright;
And, in the Shades of Heav'n, prepar'd for Light.   [*Exit Ghost.*

Almanz. O Heav'n, how dark a Riddle's thy Decree,
Which bounds our Wills, yet seems to leave 'em free!
Since thy Fore-knowledge cannot be in vain,
Our Choice must be what thou didst first ordain.
Thus, like a Captive in an Isle confin'd,
Man walks at large, a Pris'ner of the Mind:
Wills all his Crimes, while Heav'n th' Indictment draws;
And, pleading Guilty, justifies the Laws.——
Let Fate be Fate; the Lover and the Brave
Are rank'd, at least, above the vulgar Slave.
Love makes me willing to my Death to run;
And Courage scorns the Death it cannot shun.

               Enter Almahide *with a Taper.*

Almah. My Light will sure discover those who talk.——
Who dares to interrupt my private Walk?

Almanz. He, who dares love, and for that Love must die,
And, knowing this, dares yet love on, am I.

Almah. That Love which you can hope, and I can pay,
May be receiv'd and giv'n in open Day:
My Praise and my Esteem you had before;
And you have bound your self to ask no more.

Almanz. Yes, I have bound my self; but will you take
The Forfeit of that Bond which Force did make?

Almah. You know you are from Recompence debarr'd;
But purest Love can live without Reward.

Almanz. Pure Love had need be to it self a Feast,
For, like pure Elements, 'twill nourish least.

Almah. It therefore yields the only pure Content;
For it, like Angels, needs no Nourishment.
To eat and drink can no Perfection be;
All Appetite implies Necessity.

Almanz. 'Twere well, if I could like a Spirit live:
But, do not Angels Food to Mortals give.——
What if some Demon should my Death foreshow,
Or bid me change, and to the Christians go;
Will you not think I merit some Reward,
When I my Love above my Life regard?

Almah. In such a case your Change must be allow'd;
I would, my self, dispense with what you vow'd.

Almanz. Were I to die that Hour when I possess,
This Minute shall begin my Happiness.

Almah. The thoughts of Death your Passion would remove;
Death is a cold Encouragement to Love.   *Almanz.*

Almanz. No; from my Joys I to my Death would run;
And think the Bufinefs of my Life well done.
But I fhould walk a difcontented Ghoft,
If Flefh and Blood were to no purpofe loft.

Almah. You love me not, *Almanzor*; if you did,
You would not ask what Honour muft forbid.

Almanz. And what is Honour, but a Love well hid?

Almah. Yes, 'tis the Confcience of an Act well done,
Which gives us Pow'r our own Defire to fhun.
The ftrong and fecret Curb of headlong Will;
The Self-reward of Good, and Shame of Ill.

Almanz. Thefe, Madam, are the Maxims of the Day;
When Honour's prefent, and when Love's away.
The Duty of poor Honour were too hard,
In Arms all Day, at Night to mount the Guard.
Let him in Pity, now, to Reft retire;
Let thefe foft Hours be watch'd by warm Defire.

Almah. Guards, who all Day on painful Duty keep,
In Dangers are not privileg'd to Sleep.

Almanz. And with what Dangers are you threaten'd here?
Am I, alas, a Foe for you to fear?
See, Madam, at your Feet this Enemy;   [*Kneels.*
Without your Pity and your Love I die.

Almah. Rife, rife; and do not empty Hopes purfue:
Yet think that I deny my felf, not you.

Almanz. A Happinefs fo high, I cannot bear:
My Love's too fierce, and you too killing fair.
I grow enrag'd to fee fuch Excellence:
If Words, fo much diforder'd, give Offence,
My Love's too full of Zeal to think of Senfe.
Be you like me; dull Reafon hence remove;
And tedious Forms, and give a Loofe to Love.
Love eagerly; let us be Gods to Night;
And do not, with half yielding, dafh Delight.

Almah. Thou ftrong Seducer, Opportunity!
Of Womankind, half are undone by thee!
Though I refolve I will not be mifs-led,
I wifh I had not heard what you have faid!
I cannot be fo wicked to comply;
And, yet, am moft unhappy to deny!
Away.

Almanz. ———— I will not move me from this Place:
I can take no Denial from that Face!

Almah. If I could yield, (but think not that I will)
You and my felf, I in Revenge fhould kill.

For I fhould hate us both, when it were done:
And would not to the Shame of Life be won.

Alm..nz. Live but to Night, and truft to Morrow's Mind:
E'er that can come, there's a whole Life behind.
Methinks already crown'd with Joys I lye;
Speechlefs and breathlefs in an Exft fie.
Not abfent in one Thought: I am all there:
Still c'ofe, yet wifhing ftill to be more near.

Almah. Deny your own Defires; for it will be
Too little now to be deny'd by me.
Will he, who does all Great, all Noble feem,
Be loft and forfeit to his own Efteem?
Will he, who may with Heroes claim a Place,
Belie that Fame, and to himfelf be bafe?
Think how Auguft and God-like you did look,
When my Defence, unbrib'd, you undertook.
But, when an Act fo brave you difavow,
How little, and how mercenary now!

Almanz. Are, then, my Services no higher priz'd?
And can I fall fo low to be defpis'd?

Almah. Yes, for whatever may be bought, is low;
And you your felf, who fell your felf, are fo.
Remember the great Act you did this Day·
How did your Love to Virtue then give way?
When you gave Freedom to my Captive Lord;
That Rival, who poffefs'd what you ador'd.
Of fuch a Deed what Price can there be made?
Think well; is that an Action to be paid?
It was a Miracle of Virtue fhown:
And Wonders are with Wonder paid alone.
And would you all that fecret Joy of Mind,
Which great Souls only in great Actions find,
All that, for one tumultuous Minute lofe?

Almanz. I would that Minute before Ages chufe.
Praife is the Pay of Heav'n for doing good;
But Love's the beft return for Flefh and Blood.

Almah. You've mov'd my Heart fo much, I can deny
No more; but know, *Almanzor,* I can die,
Thus far my Virtue yields; if I have fhown
More Love, than what I ought, let this attone.

[*Going to ftab her felf.*

Almanz. Hold, hold!
Such fatal Proofs of Love you fhall not give:
Deny me, hate me; (both are juft) but live!
Your Virtue I will ne'er difturb again;
Nor dare to ask, for fear I fhould obtain.

Almah.

Almah. 'Tis gen'rous to have conquer'd your Desire;
You mount above your Wish, and lose it higher.
There's Pride in Virtue, and a kindly Heat:
Not Feaverish, like your Love, but full as great.
Farewel; and may our Loves hereafter be,
But Image-like, to heighten Piety.

Almanz. 'Tis time I should be gone!
Alas, I am but half converted yet:
All I resolve, I with one Look forget.
And, like a Lion, whom no Arts can tame,
Shall tear, ev'n those, who would my Rage reclaim   [*Exeunt severally.*
[*Zulema and* Hamet *watch Almanzor; and, when*
he is gone, go in after the Queen.

Enter Abdelmelech *and* Lyndaraxa.

Lyndar. It is enough; you've brought me to this Place.
Here stop, and urge no farther my Disgrace.
Kill me; in Death your Mercy will be seen,
But make me not a Captive to the Queen.

Abdelm. 'Tis therefore I this Punishment provide.
This only can revenge me on your Pride.
Prepare to suffer what you shun in vain;
And know, you are now to Obey, not Reign.

Enter Almahide *shrieking, her Hair loose; she runs*
over the Stage.

Almah. Help, help, O Heav'n, some help!

Enter Zulema *and* Hamet.

Zul. ———— Make haste before,
And intercept her Passage to the Door.

Abdelm. Villains, what Act are you attempting here!

Almah. I thank thee, Heav'n; some Succour does appear.
[*As* Abdelmelech *is going to help the Queen,* Lyndaraxa *pulls out his Sword, and holds it.*

Abdelm. With what ill Fate my good Design is curst!

Zul. We have no time to think; dispatch him first.

Abdelm. O for a Sword!
[*They make at* Abdelmelech; *he goes off at one Door,*
while the Queen escapes at the other.

Zul. Ruin'd!

Hamet. ———— Undone!

Lyndar. And, which is worst of all,
He escap'd.

Zul. ———— I hear 'em loudly call.

Lyndar. Your Fear will loose you; call as loud as they:
I have not time to teach you what to say.

The

The Court will, in a Moment, all be here;
But second what I say, and do not fear.
Call Help; run that Way; leave the rest to me.

[*Zulema and Hamet retire, and within cry help.*

Enter at several Doors, the King, Abenamar, Selin, Ozmyn,
Almanzor, *with Guards attending* Boabdelin.

Boab. What can the Cause of all this Tumult be?
And what the meaning of that naked Sword?

Lyndar. I'll tell, when Fear will so much Breath afford.
The Queen and *Abdelmelech.*————'Twill not out————
Ev'n I, who saw it, of the Truth yet doubt,
It seems so strange.

Almanz. ————Did she not name the Queen!
Haste; speak.

Lyndar. ———— How dare I speak what I have seen!
With *Hamet,* and with *Zulema* I went
To pay both theirs, and my Acknowledgment
To *Almahide;* and by her Mouth implore
Your Clemency, our Fortunes to restore,
We chose this Hour, which we believ'd most free,
When she retir'd from Noise and Company.
The Anti-chamber past, we gently knock'd,
(Unheard it seems) but found the Lodgings lock'd,
In duteous Silence while we waited there,
We, first a Noise, and then long Whispers hear.
Yet thought it was the Queen at Pray'rs alone,
'Till she distinctly said,————If this were known,
My Love, what Shame, what Danger would ensue!
Yet I (and sigh'd) could venture more for you!

Boab. O Heav'n, what do I hear! (*Almanzor*) let her go on.

Lyndar. And how? (then murmur'd in a bigger Tone
Another Voice) and how should it be known?
This Hour is from your Court Attendants free;
The King suspects *Almanzor,* but not me.   [*Zulema at the Door.*
I find her drift; *Hamet,* be confident;
Second her Words, and fear not the Event.

·— . *Zulema and* Hamet *enter. The King embraces them.*

Boab. Welcome, my only Friends; behold in me,
O Kings, behold th' Effects of Clemency!
See here the Gratitude of pardon'd Foes!
That Life I gave 'em, they for me expose!

Hamet. Though *Abdelmelech* was our Friend before,
When Duty call'd us he was so no more.

Almanz. Damn your Delay, you Torturers proceed,
I will not hear one Word, but *Almahide.*

Boab. When you, within, the Traitor's Voice did hear,
What did you then?

Zul. ————I durſt not truſt my Ear;
But, peeping through the Key-hole, I eſpy'd
The Queen; and *Abdelmelech* by her Side:
She on the Couch, he on her Boſom lay,
Her Hand about his Neck his Head did ſtay,
And from his Forehead wip'd the Drops away.

Boab. Go on, go on, my Friends, to clear my Doubt;
I hope I ſhall have Life to hear you out.

Zul. What had been, Sir, you may ſuſpect too well;
What follow'd, Modeſty forbids to tell:
Seeing, what we had thought beyond Belief,
Our Hearts ſo ſwell'd with Anger and with Grief,
That, by plain Force, we ſtrove the Door to break.
He, fearful, and with Guilt, or Love, grown weak,
Juſt as we enter'd, 'ſcap'd the other Way;
Nor did th'amazed Queen behind him ſtay.

Lyndar. His Sword, in ſo much Haſte, he could not mind,
But left this Witneſs of his Crime behind.

Boab. O proud, ingrateful, faithleſs Womankind!
How chang'd, and what a Monſter am I made!
My Love, my Honour, ruin'd and betray'd!

Almanz. Your Love and Honour! Mine are ruin'd worſe:
Furies and Hell! What right have you to curſe?
Dull Husband as you are,————
What can your Love, or what your Honour be!
I am her Lover, and ſhe's falſe to me.

Boab. Go; when the Authors of my Shame are found,
Let 'em be taken inſtantly, and bound:
They ſhall be puniſh'd as our Laws require:
'Tis juſt, that Flames ſhould be condemn'd to Fire.
This, with the Dawn of Morning, ſhall be done.

Aben. You haſte, too much, her Execution.
Her Condemnation ought to be deferr'd:
With Juſtice, none can be condemn'd unheard.

Boab. A formal Proceſs tedious is, and long·
Beſides, the Evidence is full and ſtrong.

Lyndar. The Law demands two Witneſſes· and ſhe
Is caſt (for which Heav'n knows I grieve) by three.

Ozm. Hold, Sir, ſince you ſo far inſiſt on Law,
We can, from thence, one juſt Advantage draw:
That Law, which dooms Adult'reſſes to die,
Gives Champions, too, to ſlander'd Chaſtity.

Almanz. And how dare you, who from my Bounty live,
Intrench upon my Love's Prerogative.

Your

Your Courage in your own Concernments try;
Brothers are things remote, while I am by.

Ozm. I knew not you thus far her Cause would own;
And must not suffer you to fight alone:
Let two to two in equal Combat join;
You vindicate her Person, I her Line.

Lyndar. Of all Mankind *Almanzor* has least right
In her Defence, who wrong'd his Love, to fight.

Almanz. 'Tis false; she is not ill, nor can she be;
She must be Chaste, because she's lov'd by me.

Zul. Dare you, what Sense and Reason prove, deny?

Almanz. When she's in question, Sense and Reason lie.

Zul. For Truth, for my injur'd Soveraign,
What I have said, I will to Death maintain.

Ozm. So foul a Falshood, whoe'er justifies,
Is basely born; and, like a Villain, lies.
In witness of that Truth, be this my Gage.
                                        [*Takes a Ring from his Finger.*

Hamet. I take it; and despise a Traitor's Rage.

Boab. The Combat's yours; a Guard the Lists surround,
Then raise a Scaffold in th'incompass'd Ground,
And, by it, Piles of Wood; in whose just Fire,
Her Champions slain, th'Adult'ress shall expire.

Aben. We ask no Favour, but what Arms will yield.

Boab. Chuse, then, two equal Judges of the Field:
Next Morning shall decide the doubtful Strife,
Condemn th'unchaste, or quit the virtuous Wife.

Almanz. But I am both ways curss'd.——
For *Almahide* must die, if I am slain;
Or, for my Rival I the Conquest gain.
                                        [*Exeunt.*

ACT V.

Almanzor solus.

I Have out-fac'd my self, and justify'd
What I knew false, to all the World beside.
She was as faithless as her Sex could be;
And, now I am alone, she's so to me,
She's fall'n! and, now, where shall we Virtue find?
She was the last that stood, of Womankind.
Could she so holily my Flames remove;
And fall that Hour to *Abdelmelech's* Love?
Yet her Protection I must undertake;
Not now for Love, but for my Honour's sake.

That

That mov'd me firft, and muft oblige me ftill:
My Caufe is good, however hers be ill.
I'll leave her, when fhe's freed; and let it be
Her Punifhment, fhe could be falfe to me.

    To him Abdelmelech *guarded.*

 Abdelm. Heav'n is not Heav'n, nor are there Deities.
There is fome new Rebellion in the Skies.
All that was Good and Holy is dethron'd,
And Luft and Rapine are for Juftice own'd.

 Almanz. 'Tis true, what Juftice in that Heav'n can be,
Which thus affronts me with the Sight of thee?
Why muft I be from juft Revenge debarr'd?
Chains are thy Arms, and Prifons are thy Guard:
The Death thou dy'ft may, to a Husband, be
A Satisfaction; but 'tis none to me.
My Love would Juftice to it felf afford;
But now thou creep'ft to Death, below my Sword.

 Abdelm. This Threatning would fhow better, were I free.

 Almanz. No, wert thou freed, I would not threaten thee:
This Arm fhould then.———But now it is too late!———
I could redeem thee to a nobler Fate.
As fome huge Rock,
Rent from its Quarry, does the Waves divide,
So I———
Would fowze upon thy Guards, and dafh 'em wide.
Then, to my Rage left naked and alone,
Thy too much Freedom thou fhould'ft foon bemoan:
Dar'd, like a Lark, that on the open Plain,
Purfu'd and cuff'd, feeks Shelter now in vain;
So on the Ground would'ft thou expecting lye,
Not daring to afford me Victory.
But yet thy Fate's not ripe; it is decreed,
Before thou dy'ft, that *Almahide* be freed.
My Honour firft her Danger muft remove,
And then revenge on thee my injur'd Love.   [*Exeunt feverally.*

  The Scene changes to the Vivarambla, *and appears fill'd with*
    Spectators: *A Scaffold hung with Black,* &c.

   Enter the Queen guarded, with Efperanza.

 Almah. See how the gazing People crowd the Place,
All gaping to be fill'd with my Difgrace.   [*A Shout within.*
That Shout, like the hoarfe Peals of Vultures rings,
When, over fighting Fields, they beat their Wings.
Let never Woman truft in Innocence,
Or think her Chaftity its own Defence.

        R   Mine

Mine has betray'd me to this publick Shame:
And Virtue, which I ferv'd, is but a Name.

Efper. Leave then that Shadow, and for Succour fly
To him we ferve, the Chriftians Deity.
Virtue's no God, nor has fhe Pow'r Divine:
But he protects it, who did firft enjoin.
Truft, then, in him; and, from his Grace, implore
Faith to believe, what rightly we adore.

Almah. Thou Pow'r unknown, if I have err'd, forgive:
My Infancy was taught what I believe.
But if thy Chriftians truly worfhip thee,
Let me thy Godhead in thy Succour fee:
So fhall thy Juftice in my Safety fhine,
And all my Days, which thou fhalt add, be thine.

Enter the King, Abenamar, Lyndaraxa, Benzayda: *Then* Abdelmelech *guarded. And after him* Selin *and* Alabez, *as Judges of
the Field.*

Boab. You Judges of the Field, firft take your Place.
Th'Accufers and Accus'd bring Face to Face.
Set Guards, and let the Lifts be open'd wide;
And may juft Heav'n affift the jufter Side.

Almah. What, not one tender Look, one paffing Word?
Farewel, my much unkind, but ftill lov'd Lord.
Your Throne was for my humble Fate too high,
And therefore Heav'n thinks fit that I fhould die.
My Story be forgot, when I am dead;
Left it fhould fright fome other from your Bed:
And, to forget me, may you foon adore
Some happier Maid, (yet none could love you more.)
But may you never think me innocent;
Left it fhould caufe you Trouble to repent.

Boab. 'Tis pity fo much Beauty fhould not live;   [*Afide.*
Yet I too much am injur'd to forgive.   [*Goes to his Seat.*

Trumpets: Then enter two Moors *bearing two naked Swords before
the Accufers* Zulema *and* Hamet, *who follow them. The Judges
feat themfelves; the Queen and* Abdelmelech *are led to the Scaffold.*

Alabez. Say for what End you thus in Arms appear:
What are your Names, and what demand you here?

Zul. The Zegrys ancient Race our Lineage claims;
And Zulema and Hamet are our Names.
Like Loyal Subjects in thefe Lifts we ftand,
And Juftice in our King's Behalf demand.

Hamet. For whom, in witnefs of what both have feen,
Bound by our Duty, we appeach the Queen
And Abdelmelech, of Adultery.

Zul. Which, like true Knights, we will maintain, or die.

Alabez.

Alabez. Swear on the *Alcoran* your Caufe is right;
And *Mahomet* fo profper you in Fight.
      [*They touch their Foreheads with the Alcoran, and bow*

*Trumpets on the other fide of the Stage; two Moors as before,
with bare Swords before* Almanzor *and* Ozmyn.

Selin. Say for what End you thus in Arms appear:
What are your Names, and what demand you here?
      Almanz. Ozmyn is his, *Almanzor* is my Name,
We come as Champions of the Queen's fair Fame.
      Ozm. To prove thefe *Zegrys,* like falfe Traitors, lie,
Which, like true Knights, we will maintain, or die.
            Selin *to* Almahide
Madam, do you for Champions take thefe two;
By their Succefs to live or die?
      Almah. ——————————I do.
      Selin. Swear on the *Alcoran* your Caufe is right;
And *Mahomet* fo profper you in Fight.   [*They kifs the* Alcoran.
      [Ozmyn *and* Benzayda *Embrace, and take Leave in dumb
            fhow; while* Lyndaraxa *fpeaks to her Brothers.*
      Lyndar. If you o'ercome, let neither of them live;
But ufe, with Care, th'Advantages I give·
One of their Swords in Fight fhall ufelefs be;
The Bearer of it is fuborn'd by me.   [*She and* Benzayda *retire.*
      Alabez. Now, Principals and Seconds, all advance,
And each of you affift his Fellow's Chance.
      Selin. The Wind and Sun we equally divide;
So, let th'Event of Arms the Truth decide.
The Chances of the Fight, and ev'ry Wound,
The Trumpets, on the Victor's part, refound.

      [*The Trumpets found;* Almanzor *and* Zulema *meet and fight;*
      Ozmyn *and* Hamet, *after fome Paffes, the Sword of Oz-
      myn breaks; he retires defending himfelf, and is wounded;
      the* Zegrys *Trumpets found their Advantage;* Almanzor,
      in the mean time, drives Zulema *to the farther end of the
      Stage; 'till, hearing the Trumpets of the adverfe Party,
      he looks back and fees* Ozmyn's *Misfortune; he makes at*
      Zulema *juft as* Ozmyn *falls, in retiring, and* Hamet *is
      thrufting at him.*

            Hamet *to* Ozmyn *thrufting.*
Our Diff'rence now fhall foon determin'd be.
      Almanz. Hold, Traitor, and defend thy felf from me.

[Hamet *leaves* Ozmyn, (*who cannot rife,*) *and both he and Zulema fall on* Almanzor, *and prefs him; he retires, and Hamet, advancing firft, is run through the Body and falls.
The Queen's Trumpets found.* Almanzor *purfues* Zulema.

Lyndar. I muft make hafte fome Remedy to find ———
Treafon, *Almanzor,* Treafon; look behind.

[Almanzor *looks behind him to fee who calls, and* Zulema *takes
the Advantage and Wounds him; the* Zegrys *Trumpets
found.* Almanzor *turns upon* Zulema *and Wounds him; he
falls. The Queen's Trumpets found.*

Almanz. Now Triumph in thy Sifter's Treachery. [*Stabbing him.*
Zul. Hold, hold; I have enough to make me die.
But, that I may in Peace refign my Breath,
I muft confefs my Crime before my Death.
Mine is the Guilt, the Queen is innocent ·
I lov'd her; and, to compafs my Intent,
Us'd Force; which *Abdelmelech* did prevent.
The Lie my Sifter forg'd: But, O! my Fate
Comes on too foon, and I repent too late.
Fair Queen, forgive, and let my Penitence
Expiate fome part of———   [*Dies.*
Almah. ——— Ev'n thy whole Offence!
          Almanzor *to the Judges.*
If ought remains in the Sultana's Caufe,
I here am ready to fulfil the Laws.
Selin. The Law is fully fatisfy'd, and we
Pronounce the Queen and *Abdelmelech* free.
Abdelm. Heav'n thou art juft!

[*The Judges rife from their Seats, and go before* Almanzor *to the
Queen's Scaffold, he unbinds the Queen and* Abdelmelech, *they all
go off, the People fhouting, and the Trumpets founding the while.*

Boab. Before we pay our Thanks, or fhow our Joy;
Let us our needful Charity employ.
Some fkilful Surgeon fpeedily be found,
T'apply fit Remedies to *Ozmyn's* Wound.
          Benzayda *running to* Ozmyn.
That be my Charge, my Linnen I will tear·
Wafh it with Tears, and bind it with my Hair.
Ozm. With how much Pleafure I my Pains endure!
And blefs the Wound which caufes fuch a Cure.
          [*Exit* Ozmyn, *led by* Benzayda *and* Abenamar.
Boab. Some from the Place of Combat bear the Slain:
Next *Lyndaraxa's* Death I fhould ordain:
But let her, who this Mifchief did contrive,
For ever banifh'd from *Granada* live.

Lyndar. Thou fhou'dft have punifh'd more, or not at all ·
By her thou haft not ruin'd, thou fhalt fall.   [*Afide.*
The *Zegrys* fhall revenge their branded Line   -
Betray their Gate, and with the Chriftians join.
       [*Exit* Lyndaraxa *with* Alabez; *the Bodies of her Brothers*
       are born after her.
      Almanzor, Almahide, Efperanza *re-enter to the King.*
   Almah. The Thanks thus paid, which firft to Heav'n were due,
My next, *Almanzor,* let me pay to you:
Somewhat there is, of more Concernment, too,
Which 'tis not fit you fhould, in publick, know.
Firft let your Wounds be drefs'd with fpeedy Care, ,
And then you fhall th' important Secret fhare.
   Almanz. When e'er you fpeak,
Were my Wounds Mortal, they fhould ftill bleed on;
And I would liften 'till my Life were gone:
My Soul fhould, ev'n for your laft Accent, ftay;
And then fhout out, and with fuch fpeed obey,
It fhould not Bait at Heav'n to ftop its Way.   [*Exit Almanz.*
   Boab. Tis true, *Almanzor* did her Honour fave;   [*Afide.*
But yet what private Bufinefs can they have!
Such Freedom Virtue will not fure allow;
I cannot clear my Heart; but muft my Brow:
       He approaches Almahide.
Welcome again my Virtuous, Loyal Wife;
Welcome to Love, to Honour, and to Life.——
       [*Goes to Salute her, fhe ftarts back.*
You feem————————
As if you from a loath'd Embrace did go!
   Almah. Then briefly will I fpeak, (fince you muft know
What to the World my future Acts will fhow:)
But hear me firft, and then my Reafons weigh:
'Tis known how Duty led me to obey
My Father's Choice; and how I fince did live,
You, Sir, can beft your Teftimony give.
How to your Aid I have *Almanzor* brought,
When by rebellious Crowds your Life was fought;
Then, how I bore your caufelefs Jealoufie,
(For I muft fpeak) and after fet you free,
When you were Pris'ner in the Chance of War;
Thefe, fure, are Proofs of Love.————
   Boab. ———— I grant they are.
   Almah. And could you, then, O cruelly unkind,
So ill reward fuch Tendernefs of Mind!
Could you, denying what our Laws afford
The meaneft Subject, on a Traitor's Word,

                                     Unheard

Unheard, condemn, and suffer me to go
To Death, and yet no common Pity show!

   Boab. Love fill'd my Heart ev'n to the Brim before;
And then, with too much Jealousie, boil'd o'er.

   Almah. Be't Love or Jealousie, 'tis such a Crime,
That I'm forewarn'd to trust a second time.
Know then, my Pray'rs to them shall never cease
To Crown your Arms with War, your Wars with Peace:
But, from this Day, I will not know your Bed.
Though *Almahide* still lives, your Wife is dead:
And, with her, dies a Love so pure and true,
It could be kill'd by nothing but by you.   [*Exit* Almahide

   Boab. Yes, you will spend your Life in Pray'rs for me,
And yet this Hour my hated Rival see.
She might a Husband's Jealousie forgive;
But she will only for *Almanzor* live.
It is resolv'd, I will, my self, provide
That Vengeance, which my useless Laws deny'd ·
And, by *Almanzor*'s Death, at once, remove
The Rival of my Empire, and my Love.

                                 [*Exit* Boabdelin.

   Enter Almahide, *led by* Almanzor, *and follow'd by* Esperanza,
                She speaks entring.

   Almah. How much, *Almanzor,* to your Aid I owe,
Unable to repay, I blush to know.
Yet, forc'd by Need, e'er I can clear that Score,
I, like ill Debtors, come to borrow more.

   Almanz. Your new Commands I on my Knees attend:
I was created for no other end.
Born to be yours, I do, by Nature, serve;
And, like the lab'ring Beast, no Thanks deserve.

   Almah. Yet first your Virtue to your Succour call,
For, in this hard Command, you'll need it all.

   Almanz. I stand prepar'd; and whatsoe'er it be,
Nothing is hard to him who loves like me.

   Almah. Then know, I from your Love must yet implore
One Proof: ———that you would never see me more.
              Almanzor *starting back*

   I must confess,
For this last Stroke I did no Guard provide;
I could suspect no Foe was near that Side
From Winds and thick'ning Clouds we Thunder fear:
None dread it from that Quarter which is clear.
And I would fain believe, 'tis but your Art
To shew
You knew where deepest you could wound my Heart.

                                Almah.

Almah. So much Respect is to your Passion due,
That sure I could not practise Arts on you.
But, that you may not doubt what I have said,
This Hour I have renounc'd my Husband's Bed:
Judge then how much my Fame would injur'd be,
If, leaving him, I should a Lover see!

Almanz. If his Unkindness have deserv'd that Curse,
Must I, for loving well, be punish'd worse?

Almah. Neither your Love nor Merits I compare;
But my unspotted Name must be my Care.

Almanz. I have this Day establish'd its Renown.

Almah. Would you so soon, what you have rais'd, throw down?

Almanz. But, Madam, is not yours a greater Guilt,
To ruin him who has that Fabrick built?

Almah. No Lover should his Mistress Pray'rs withstand:
Yet you contemn my absolute Command.

Almanz. 'Tis not Contempt,
When your Command is issu'd out too late:
'Tis past my Pow'r, and all beyond is Fate,
I scarce could leave you, when to Exile sent;
Much less, when now recall'd from Banishment:
For if that Heat your Glances cast were strong;
Your Eyes, like Glasses, fire, when held so long.

Almah. Then, since you needs will all my Weakness know,
I love you, and so well, that you must go:
I am so much oblig'd, and have, withal,
A Heart so boundless and so prodigal,
I dare not trust my self, or you, to stay;
But, like frank Gamesters, must forswear the Play.

Almanz. Fate, thou art kind, to strike so hard a Blow;
I am quite stunn'd, and past all Feeling, now.
Yet——can you tell me you have Pow'r and Will
To save my Life, and, at that instant, kill?

Almah. This, had you stay'd, you never must have known:
But, now you go, I may with Honour own.

Almanz. But, Madam, I am forc'd to disobey:
In your Defence my Honour bids me stay.
I promis'd to secure your Life and Throne,
And, Heav'n be thank'd, that Work is yet undone.

Almah. I here make void that Promise which you made;
For now I have no farther need of Aid.
That Vow, which to my plighted Lord was giv'n,
I must not break; but may transfer to Heav'n:
I will with Vestals live:
There needs no Guard at a Religious Door;
Few will disturb the Praying and the Poor.

Almanz.

Almanz. Let me but near that happy Temple stay,
And, through the Grates, peep on you once a Day;
To famish'd Hope I would no Banquet give:
I cannot starve, and wish but just to live.
Thus, as a drowning Man
Sinks often, and does still more faintly rise,
With his last Hold catching whate'er he spies;
So, fall'n from those proud Hopes I had before,
Your Aid I for a dying Wretch implore.
    Almah. I cannot your hard Destiny withstand;
                Boabdelin and Guards above.
But slip, like bending Rushes, from your Hand.
Sink all at once, since you must sink at last.
    Almanz. Can you that last Relief of Sight remove,
And thrust me out the utmost Line of Love!
Then, since my Hopes of Happiness are gone,
Deny'd all Favours, I will seize this one.
                      [Catches her Hand and kisses it.
    Boab. My just Revenge no longer I'll forbear.
I've seen too much; I need not stay to hear.   *[Descends.*
    Almanz. As a small Shower
To the parch'd Earth does some Refreshment give,
So, in the Strength of this, one Day I'll live:
A Day,——a Year,——an Age,——for ever, now;
    [Betwixt each Word he kisses her Hand by force; she struggling.
I feel from ev'ry Touch a new Soul flow.
                    [She snatches her Hand away.
My hop'd Eternity of Joy is past!
'Twas insupportable, and could not last.
Were Heav'n not made of less, or duller Joy,
'Twould break each Minute, and it self destroy.
            Enter King and Guards below.
    Boab. This, this is he, for whom thou didst deny
To share my Bed:——Let 'em together die.
    Almah. Hear me, my Lord.
    Boab. ————Your flatt'ring Arts are vain:
Make haste; and execute what I ordain.   *[To the Guards.*
    Almanz. Cut piece-meal, in this Cause,
From ev'ry Wound I should new Vigour take.
And ev'ry Limb should new *Almanzors* make.
          *[He puts himself before the Queen, the
            Guards attack him, with the King.*
        Enter Abdelmelech.
    Abdelm. What angry God, to exercise his Spight,   *[To the King.*
Has arm'd your left Hand, to cut off your right?
         [The King turns, and the Fight ceases.
                    Haste,

Hafte, not to give, but to prevent a Fate:
The Foes are enter'd at th'*Elvira* Gate:
Falfe *Lyndaraxa* has the Town betray'd,
And all the *Zegrys* give the *Spaniards* Aid.

   Boab. O Mifchief, not fufpected nor forefeen!

   Abdelm. Already they have gain'd the *Zacatin,*
And, thence, the *Vivarambla* Place poffeft.
While our faint Soldiers fcarce defend the reft.
The Duke of *Arcos* does one Squadron head;
The next by *Ferdinand* himfelf is led.

   Almah. Now, brave *Almanzor,* be a God again;
Above our Crimes and your own Paffions reign.
My Lord has been, by Jealoufie, mifs-led,
To think I was not faithful to his Bed.
I can forgive him, though my Death he fought,
For too much Love can never be a Fault.
Protect him, then; and, what to his Defence
You give not, give to clear my Innocence.

   Almanz. Liften, fweet Heav'n; and, all ye Blefs'd above,
Take Rules of Virtue from a Mortal Love.
You've rais'd my Soul; and, if it mount more high,
'Tis as the Wren did on the Eagle fly.
Yes, I once more will my Revenge neglect:
And, whom you can forgive, I can protect.

   Boab. How hard a Fate is mine, ftill doom'd to Shame;
I make Occafions for my Rival's Fame! [*Exeunt. An Alarm within.*
     Enter Ferdinand, Ifabella, Don Alonzo d'Aguilar,
        Spaniards *and Ladies.*

   K. *Ferd.* Already more than half the Town is gain'd:
But there is yet a doubtful Fight maintain'd.

   Alonzo. The fierce young King the enter'd does attack,
And the more fierce *Almanzor* drives 'em back.

   K. *Ferd.* The valiant *Moors* like raging Lions fight;
Each Youth encourag'd by his Lady's Sight.

   Q. *Ifabel.* I will advance with fuch a fhining Train,
That *Moorifh* Beauties fhall oppofe in vain:
Into the Prefs of clafhing Swords we'll go;
And, where the Darts fly thickeft, feek the Foe.

   K. *Ferd.* May Heav'n, which has infpir'd this gen'rous Thought,
Avert thofe Dangers you have boldly fought.
Call up more Troops; the Women, to our Shame,
Will ravifh from the Men their Part of Fame.
               [*Exeunt* Ifabella *and Ladies.*
     Enter Alabez, *and kiffes the King's Hand.*

   Alabez. Fair *Lyndaraxa,* and the *Zegry* Line,
Have led their Forces with your Troops to join.

S

                           The

The adverfe Part, which obftinately fought,
Are broke; and *Abdelmelech* Pris'ner brought.

K. *Ferd.* Fair *Lyndaraxa,* and her Friends, fhall find
Th'Effects of an oblig'd and grateful Mind.

Alabez. But, marching by the *Vivarambla* Place,
The Combat carry'd a more doubtful face:
In that vaft Square the *Moors* and *Spaniards* met;
Where the fierce Conflict is continu'd yet.
But with Advantage on the adverfe Side,
Whom fierce *Almanzor* does to Conqueft guide.

K. *Ferd.* With my *Caftilian* Foot I'll meet his Rage;

[*Is going out: Shouts within are heard,* Victoria, Victoria.

But thefe loud Clamours better News prefage.

Enter the Duke of Arcos, *and Soldiers; their Swords*
drawn and bloody.

D. *Arcos. Granada* now is yours; and there remain
No *Moors,* but fuch as own the Pow'r of *Spain.*
That Squadron, which their King in Perfon led,
We charg'd, but found *Almanzor* in their Head.
Three fev'ral times we did the *Moors* attack,
And thrice, with Slaughter, did he drive us back.
Our Troops then fhrunk; and ftill we loft more Ground,
'Till from our Queen, we needful Succour found.
Her Guards to our Affiftance bravely flew,
And, with frefh Vigour, did the Fight renew.
At the fame time————————
Did *Lyndaraxa* with her Troops appear,
And, while we charg'd the Front, ingag'd the Rear.
Then fell the King, (flain by a *Zegry*'s Hand:)

K. *Ferd.* How could he fuch united Force withftand?

D. *Arcos.* Difcourag'd with his Death, the *Moorifh* Pow'rs
Fell back; and, falling back, were prefs'd by ours.
But, as when Winds and Rain together croud,
They fwell 'till they have burft the bladder'd Cloud;
And firft the Lightning, flafhing deadly clear,
Flies, falls, confumes, e'er it does appear:
So, from his fhrinking Troops, *Almanzor* flew;
Each Blow gave Wounds, and with each Wound he flew.
His Force at once I envy'd and admir'd;
And, rufhing forward, where my Men retir'd,
Advanc'd alone.

K. *Ferd.* ————————You hazarded too far
Your Perfon, and the Fortune of the War.

D. *Arcos.* Already both our Arms for Fight did bare,
Already held 'em threatning in the Air:

When

When Heav'n (it muſt be Heav'n) my Sight did guide
To view his Arm, upon whoſe Wriſt I ſpy'd
A Ruby Croſs in Diamond Bracelets ty'd.
And juſt above it, in the brawnier part,
By Nature was engrav'd a bloody Heart.
Struck with theſe Tokens, which ſo well I knew.
And ſtagg'ring back, ſome Paces I withdrew;
He follow'd, and ſuppos'd it was my Fear:
When, from above, a ſhrill Voice reach'd his Ear;
Strike not thy Father, it was heard to cry;
Amaz'd, and caſting round his wond'ring Eye,
He ſtopp'd; then, thinking that his Fears were vain,
He lifted up his thund'ring Arm again:
Again the Voice with-held him from my Death:
Spare, ſpare his Life, it cry'd, who gave thee Breath.
Once more he ſtopp'd; then threw his Sword away ;
Bleſs'd Shade, he ſaid, I hear thee, I obey
Thy ſacred Voice; then, in the ſight of all,
He at my Feet, I on his Neck did fall.

    K. Ferd. O bleſs'd Event!————

    D. Arcos. ———— The *Moors* no longer fought;
But all their Safety, by Submiſſion, fought:
Mean time my Son grew faint with loſs of Blood:
And, on his bending Sword ſupported, ſtood,
Yet, with a Voice beyond his Strength, he cry'd,
Lead me to live, or die, by *Almahide.*

    K. Ferd. I am not for his Wounds leſs griev'd than you.
For if, what now my Soul divines, proves true,
This is that Son, whom in his Infancy
You loſt, when by my Father forc'd to fly.

    D. Arcos. His Siſter's Beauty did my Paſſion move,
(The Crime for which I ſuffer'd was my Love)
Our Marriage known, to Sea we took our Flight;
There, in a Storm, *Almanzor* firſt ſaw Light.
On his right Arm, a bloody Heart was grav'd,
(The Mark by which, this Day, my Life was ſav'd.)
The Bracelets and the Croſs, his Mother ty'd
About his Wriſt, e'er ſhe in Child-bed dy'd.
How we were Captives made, when ſhe was dead;
And how *Almanzor* was in *Africk* bred,
Some other Hour you may at leiſure hear,
For ſee, the Queen, in Triumph, does appear.

   Enter Queen Iſabella, Lyndaraxa, *Ladies,* Moors *and* Spaniards *mix'd*
     as Guards. Abdelmelech, Abenamar, Selin, *Priſoners.*
      King Ferdinand *Embracing Queen* Iſabella.

    All Stories, which *Granada's* Conqueſt tell,
Shall Celebrate the Name of *Iſabel.*   S 2   Your

Your Ladies too, who, in their Country's Caufe,
Led on the Men, fhall fhare in your Applaufe·
And for your fakes, henceforward, I ordain,
No Lady's Dow'r fhall queftion'd be in *Spain*.
Fair *Lyndaraxa*, for the Help fhe lent,
Shall, under Tribute, have this Government.

 Abdelm. O Heav'n, that I fhould live to fee this Day !
 Lyndar. You murmur now, but you fhall foon obey.
I knew this Empire to my Fate was ow'd:
Heav'n held it back as long as e'er it could.
For thee, bafe Wretch, I want a Torture yet—— [*To* Abdelm.
——I'll Cage thee, thou fhalt be my *Bajazet*.
I on no Pavement but on thee will tread;
And, when I mount, my Foot fhall know thy Head.
        [Abdelm. *ftabbing her with a Ponyard.*
 This firft fhall know thy Heart.
 Lyndar. ————————— O! I am Slain!
 Abdelm. Now boaft, thy Country is betray'd to *Spain*.
 K. *Ferd.* Look to the Lady.——Seize the Murderer.
        [Abdelm. *ftabbing himfelf.*
I'll do my felf that Juftice I did her.
Thy Blood I to thy ruin'd Country give, [*To* Lyndar.
But love too well thy Murther to out-live.
Forgive a Love, excus'd by its excefs,
Which, had it not been cruel, had been lefs.
Condemn my Paffion, then, but pardon me;
And think I murder'd him, who murder'd thee. [*Dies.*
 Lyndar. Die for us both; I have not leifure now;
A Crown is come, and will not Fate allow:
And yet I feel fomething, like Death, is near:
My Guards, my Guards;————
Let not that ugly Skeleton appear.
Sure Deftiny miftakes, this Death's not mine;
She dotes, and meant to cut another Line.
Tell her I am a Queen;———— but 'tis too late;
Dying, I charge Rebellion on my Fate:
Bow down ye Slaves———— [*To the* Moors.
Bow quickly down, and your Submiffion fhow. [*They bow.*
I'm pleas'd to tafte an Empire e'er I go. [*Dies.*
 Selin. She's dead, and here her proud Ambition ends.
 Aben. Such Fortune ftill fuch black Defigns attends.
 K. *Ferd.* Remove thofe mournful Objects from our Eyes,
And fee perform'd their Fun'ral Obfequies.

      [*The Bodies carry'd off.*

      Enter

Enter Almanzor *and* Almahide, Ozmyn *ana* Benzayda. Almahide
brought in a Chair Almanzor *led betwixt Soldiers ·* Isabella *Salutes*
Almahide *in dumb show.*

Duke of Arcos *presenting* Almanzor *to the King.*
See here that Son, whom I with Pride call mine,
And who dishonours not your Royal Line.

K. *Ferd.* I'm now secure, this Scepter, which I gain,
Shall be continu'd in the Pow'r of *Spain*,
Since he, who could alone my Foes defend,
By Birth and Honour is become my Friend.
Yet I can own no Joy, nor Conquest boast,   [*To* Almanzor.
While in this Blood I see how dear it cost.

Almanz. This Honour to my Veins new Blood will bring:
Streams cannot fail, fed by so high a Spring:
But all Court-Customs I so little know,
That I may fail in those Respects I owe.
I bring a Heart which Homage never knew;
Yet it finds something of it self in you ·
Something so kingly, that my haughty Mind
Is drawn to yours, because 'tis of a Kind.

Q. *Isabel.* And yet, that Soul, which bears its self so high,
If Fame be true, admits a Sovereignty.
This Queen, in her fair Eyes, such Fetters brings,
As Chain that Heart, which scorns the Pow'r of Kings.

Almah. Little of Charm in these sad Eyes appears;
If they had any, now 'tis lost in Tears.
A Crown, and Husband, ravish'd in one Day,
Excuse a Grief, I cannot chuse but Pay.

Q. *Isabel.* Have Courage, Madam, Heav'n has Joys in store
To recompence those Losses you deplore.

Almah. I know your God can all my Woes-redress;
To him I made my Vows in my Distress.
And, what a Misbeliever vow'd this Day,
Though not a Queen, a Christian yet shall pay.

Queen Isabella *Embracing her.*
That Christian Name you shall receive from me;
And *Isabella* of *Granada* be.

Benz. This blessed Change we all with Joy receive;
And beg to learn that Faith which you believe.

Q. *Isabel.* With Rev'rence for those Holy Rites prepare;
And all commit your Fortunes to my Care.

King Ferdinand *to* Almahide.
You, Madam, by that Crown you lose, may gain,
If you accept a Coronet of *Spain*;
Of which *Almanzor's* Father stands possest.

Queen Isabella *to* Almahide.
May you in him, and he in you be blest.   *Almah.*

Almah. I owe my Life and Honour to his Sword;
But owe my Love to my departed Lord.

   Almanz. Thus, when I have no living Force to dread,
Fate finds me Enemies amongst the dead.
I'm now to conquer Ghosts, and to destroy
The strong Impressions of a Bridal Joy.

   Almah. You've yet a greater Foe, than these can be;
Virtue opposes you, and Modesty.

   Almanz. From a false Fear that Modesty does grow;
And thinks true Love, because 'tis fierce, its Foe.
'Tis but the Wax whose Seals on Virgins stay:
Let it approach Love's Fire, 'twill melt away.
But I have liv'd too long; I never knew,
When Fate was conquer'd, I must Combat you.
I thought to climb the steep Ascent of Love;
But did not think to find a Foe above.
'Tis time to die, when you my Bar must be,
Whose Aid alone could give me Victory.
Without———
I'll pull up all the Sluces of the Flood:
And Love, within, shall boil out all my Blood.

   Q. *Isabel.* Fear not your Love should find so sad Success;
While I have Pow'r to be your Patroness.
I am her Parent, now, and may command
So much of Duty, as to give her Hand.

                      [*Gives him* Almahide's *Hand.*

   Almah. Madam, I never can dispute your Pow'r,
Or, as a Parent, or a Conqueror.
But, when my Year of Widdowhood expires,
Shall yield to your Command, and his Desires.

   Almanz. Move swiftly, Sun; and fly a Lover's pace;
Leave Weeks and Months behind thee in thy Race!

   K. *Ferd.* Mean time, you shall my Victories pursue,
The *Moors* in Woods and Mountains to subdue.

   Almanz. The Toils of War shall help to wear each Day,
And Dreams of Love shall drive my Nights away.
Our Banners to th' *Alhambra*'s Turrets bear;
Then, wave our conqu'ring Crosses in the Air;
And cry, with Shouts of Triumph; Live and Reign,
Great *Ferdinand* and *Isabel* of *Spain*.

EPI-

EPILOGUE

To the Second PART of

GRANADA.

THEY who have beſt ſucceeded on the Stage,
    Have ſtill conform'd their Genius to their Age.
Thus Johnſon did Mechanick Humour ſhow,
When Men were dull, and Converſation low.
Then Comedy was faultleſs, but 'twas courſe:
Cobb's Tankard was a Jeſt, and Otter's Horſe.
And, as their Comedy, their Love was mean,
Except, by chance, in ſome one labour'd Scene:
Which muſt attone for an ill-written Play.
They roſe, but at their Height could ſeldom ſtay.
Fame then was cheap; and the firſt Comer ſped:
And they have kept it ſince, by being dead.
But, were they now to write, when Criticks weigh
Each Line, and ev'ry Word, throughout a Play,
None of 'em, no not Johnſon in his Height,
Could paſs, without allowing Grains for Weight.
Think it not Envy, that theſe Truths are told;
Our Poet's not malicious, though he's bold.
'Tis not to brand 'em that their Faults are ſhown,
But, by their Errors, to excuſe his own.
If Love and Honour now are higher rais'd,
'Tis not the Poet, but the Age is prais'd.

Wit's

Wit's now arriv'd to a more high Degree;
Our native Language more refin'd and free.
Our Ladies and our Men now speak more Wit,
In Conversation, than those Poets writ.
Then, one of these is, consequently, true;
That what this Poet writes comes short of you,
And imitates you ill, (which most he fears)
Or else his Writing is not worse than theirs.
Yet, though you judge, (as sure the Criticks will)
That some before him writ with greater Skill:
In this one Praise he has their Fame surpast,
To please an Age more Gallant than the last.

FINIS.

Lightning Source UK Ltd.
Milton Keynes UK
174086UK00006B/96/P